RED'S DEVIL'S

Four women meet a mysterious man who introduces them to a world of exotic sexual pleasure. See how their sexuality blossomed into something dangerous in the darkest side of the sex industry. Can Lisa, Dara, Amber, and Brittany resist his seduction, or will these four angels become Red's Devils? Follow them on their sexual escapades as they learn and play The Game…

RED'S DEVIL'S

Chapter 1

Red, is a strong, sexy, mysterious man. He owned a strip club in Anmoore, West Virginia. He was an only child and his parents died at an early age, so he bounced around from foster home to foster home until he was 18 years old. He worked hard all of his life. Red loved women and he loved sex. He was a very sexual creature. Red had money and the style of an extraordinarily successful man. He knew what he

RED'S DEVIL'S

wanted, and he took it. The word NO was not in his vocabulary. Red made things happen. He worked hard and made the money to buy his club. His life dream is to be surrounded by beautiful exotic women of all shapes, sizes, and colors.

Red's bar was the hottest spot in West Virginia. No other bar could compete. He had the best, most beautiful dancers in the state collaborating with him. They were his girls. They were loyal to him and made him a hell of a lot of money. Red worked in real estate for years, that's how he got the club at such a great price and a great location.

Red had businessmen from all over the world frequenting his club daily. There were no slow days at Red's Devils. Every day was a good money-making day. Red's girls loved working there. He respected his girls and protected them. They were his family, something he craved his whole life. Now he had handpicked his family he would never be alone again.
He made his girls wear elegant dresses while they were on the floor. The only time they were completely nude was on stage or in the dressing

room. That was one of his rules. His number one rule was no drugs of any kind. They were not allowed to get drunk on the job either. You had to carry yourself respectfully at all times in Red's establishment. He would not accept anything less from his girls, or his family. He demanded their respect and loyalty.

The girls were not allowed to dance at any other bars or do any private shows or parties unless Red approved it. If you got caught breaking the rules your time at Red Devils is over. There were no chances! All you have is one time to fuck up and you were banned from the family for good. When and if you were banned, you were to have no contact with any of the remaining girls for any reason. It was like being voted off the island, there was no coming back from that. You betray Red and he will make sure you never make money like that ever again. That is how powerful he became over the years.

Some girls were never seen again after being dismissed from Reds Devils. Rumor has it that Red took care of the girls permanently. Truth be told you would make a big mistake by betraying him. No one knows for sure what happened to the girls. Maybe they moved away to another town or city to start a new life. No one would ever really know the truth but Red himself. Most folks didn't ask because they were too afraid to want to know the truth. Whatever the truth was, it would die with him. Other people said Red was tied in with the mafia. Others said he ran drugs out of his club. A lot of the rumors were from pure hatred, jealousy, or only plain fear. All that did was help boost his reputation as a ruthless business owner, so Red did not mind the hushed whispers about him if they were true or not. Red never admitted or denied any of the many rumors surfing around the small town and it made people respect him even more. Red could care less about what was said about him. Money and beautiful women ruled his world. For him, what a great world it was.

RED'S DEVIL'S

Chapter 2

AMBER

Amber was exceptionally beautiful. She had an exotic look like no other. She was incredibly attractive and turned more than just a few heads. She could get about anything she wanted from a man. They would do anything for her. She knew she was beautiful, and she used what she had to get what she wanted. Amber was 5 feet 2 inches and 145 pounds. She had a petite build, an hourglass figure with a nice set of voluptuous titties. Her light brown, sexy eyes were hypnotizing. She was a very, sexy red bone.

She grew up in Virginia and then moved to West Virginia where she was raised by her mom. She had a few brothers and sisters. She knew her dad, but they did not have a strong relationship. He was not really in the picture while growing up. Amber had a good mother; it was incredibly hard on her to raise several children all alone with minimum income. Amber eventually found ways to make her own money and help her mother out as much as she could. Amber learned a lot from watching her mom and taking her advice. She was book-smart and street-smart. She was a true hustler. She did not play any games or take no shit from anybody, male or female. She was small but feisty as hell. She knew how to take care of herself, her mom made sure of that. She had plenty of haters, so now she kept her pistol on her at all times.

Presently, Amber did not have any kids. She knew she was not ready for motherhood, and she promised herself that she would not bring a child into this world until she was financially stable. So, when she got pregnant by her first puppy love, she went to Charleston to have an abortion without telling her mom. She knew her mom was totally against abortions. Amber hated keeping things from her but at that time, she felt like she didn't have a choice. Amber did not want her mom to look at her and be disappointed.

When she was in high school, Amber began hustling. She started small with a couple of ounces of the weed and then moved up to selling Ex pills and Coke. She had a good connection that would come from Detroit to take care of her. So, in return, she took care of him. Fairtrade in her eyes. She made enough money to move her, her mother and her siblings into a nice house in Carolina, West Virginia. Then, at the age of 18, Amber moved out and got her own apartment. Her drug connection bought her a Grand Prix so she could move around better. Amber always had a blunt rolled or a shot in the hand and a dog on her side. Amber was small but still sexy. She knew being sexy was all about attitude, not the body type. It is all about the state of mind. No matter what a woman looks like, if she was confident, she was sexy. You can be sexy and confident in your skin no matter what size you are.

Amber had a best friend named Michelle. They grew up and went to school together. They were thicker than thieves for almost 20 years until Amber started using men to get what she wanted. Michelle was her best friend but did not agree with Amber's lifestyle, so they eventually grew apart. Amber liked sex and she was incredibly good at it. Most of all, she enjoyed it. She did not understand why people judge women for being confident in their sexuality. But men could sleep with whomever they wanted, and it would only be brushed off by saying "Oh, he's just a man." Well, fuck that. She was a woman who knew what she liked, and she was not ashamed of it. She

RED'S DEVIL'S

was a grown ass woman at that and could do what or who the hell she pleased. She gave no fucks about what anybody thought or said.

With Amber, you had to pay to play, and you better come correct with her because she was far from a cheap thrill. To her, pussy meant power. Amber used the power of the pussy to secure her bag and her future. No time for crushes, side chicks, or cuddle buddies. Her target was the 401K, and six figures or better, period. She had awfully expensive tastes and lived a very lavish lifestyle. Amber had an extremely high-profile client list of lawyers, councilmen, politicians, and even doctors. Her little black book was worth big money and it was for her eyes only. Amber worked alone. Her clients loved her and her bag of tricks. She could role-play or be a dominatrix. She was always in control. Her clients would play by her rules. She was the boss. They were to obey her every command.

Amber ran into all kinds of secret freaks, and they had freaky fantasies. This introduced Amber into the deep, dark world of S&M. Amber had levels of gratification. Everyone was not on the same level, so Amber carried herself with poise. To Amber, sex was like money, too much is never enough. Amber knew the art of seduction. She knew what men wanted and she gave it to them, slowly making them beg. Amber never loved any of her clients because she had loveless sex. Sex without love was like exercise to Amber and she loved a good workout. Had to keep that beautiful body looking good. To her, hearing a man moan her name because of her pleasuring him was the sexiest thing ever. Amber was a good girl with bad habits. She had a dirty mind but hell a dirty mind made conversations more interesting. A few of her clients tried to conquer her heart while she ruffled their sheets, but Amber wasn't having it. She was a unique woman with a dangerous combination …sexy, intelligent and a dirty mind.

One fateful day, she was buying more toys for her bags of tricks at the local sex store. Red just so happened to be out recruiting talent when she instantly caught his eye with her alluring exotic beauty. As soon as Red laid eyes on her, he knew he had to have her. He wanted Amber to be a part of his family. Red gets what he wants by any means necessary. He was willing to do whatever it took to have Amber as his own. Amber was looking at some nipple clips when Red approached her.

"My God, you are so beautiful!" Red said to Amber.

"Thank you very much" Amber looked at Red and instantly knew he was big money. He looked like big money, smelled like big money, and carried himself like big money. Amber found herself getting a little turned on by Red's sexy, powerful presence.

"I'm Amber, it's nice to meet you."

"My name is Red, have you heard of me?" He stuck his hand out to shake Amber's hand. She politely complied as he raised her hand to his mouth and planted a sexy kiss on it.

"Pleased to meet you, sweetheart."

"No, the pleasure is all mine." She replied. Of course, Amber had heard of Red.

She heard all of the rumors, she just had never met him in person. Now she was kicking herself for not meeting him sooner because Red was sexy s hell and very attractive.

Amber did not want to be owned or controlled. She was used to her own rules and being her own boss. She did fine on her own. If she became a part of his family, all that would change. Amber decided that it was not a good idea to get involved with Red. She liked things just the way they were. Amber was good at playing by her own rules.

"I am sure you have heard about my club Red Devils. I would be honored to have you join my family. It would be a great financial opportunity for you and me as well."

"Excuse me Mr. Red, but I think I will have to pass."

"As good as it sounds, I am doing simply fine."

"Are you sure about that Amber?" "I think that would be a big mistake." Amber could not tell if he was disappointed or if he was threatening her. Either way, she knew she would not be joining Red's family anytime soon.

RED'S DEVIL'S

"I'm sorry Red, thanks for the invitation but I'm going to have to pass. It was nice meeting you, but I need to be going." Amber turned to pay for her items.

"Let me get that for you. It is the least I can do for such a beautiful woman." Red pulled out his card and slid it to the cashier.

"Thank you, that's nice but I can manage it, you have a nice evening Red." Amber grabbed her bag and walked out of the store. Red watched Amber leave. No one had ever turned him down like that. There were a few girls that were hesitant but eventually gave in to a little influence but never like this. He was determined to have Amber, but he knew he would have to work a little harder to get her. He was just buying his time until she was his. He was not going to take no for an answer. If she knew what was good for her, she would wise up and become one of his devils; he would hate for such a beautiful woman to come up missing. Red watched Amber get in her car while he wrote down her license plate number. He needed to know more about this beautiful stubborn girl that turned him down.

RED'S DEVIL'S

The cashier saw the look on Red's face and could tell he was plotting something. He watched Red walk out of the door. Red was determined to find out everything he could about Amber but, for now, he had a business to run. Amber would be number one on his to-do list. Amber knew that she was on Red's most wanted list now. She could not stop thinking about all Red's money. She could still smell his sexy ass cologne. Thinking about if she made the right choice. She was not sure if she wanted to enter Red's world but now her wheels were turning. She was very skeptical yet considering a move. Amber lived the lifestyle that she created for herself. She worked hard to build up her clientele and her reputation. She was doing very well for herself. It did not make sense to change things when they were going so well. If it is not broken do not fix it. Amber did not know much about Red but what she had heard in the streets. What she did not know was how cold and calculating Red was and could be. She was about to enter a world of sex, money, and betrayal. Amber thought that Red might be cleverer than devil and twice as sexy.

Chapter 3

DARA

     Dara was born and raised in Fairmont WV with both of her parents until her father passed away while stationed overseas when she was younger. Dara had three sisters and she was the middle child. Dara was mixed; her mom is black, and her father is white. Dara was around 5 foot 4 inches a pretty redbone with brown eyes and a beautiful smile. Dara was a double D with no ass and that did not matter. Dara was still beautiful, and sexy. Her confidence was refreshing. Dara was a beautiful woman with a beautiful body good for one night, but a woman with a beautiful mind is good for a lifetime.

When Dara was younger, she was a quiet girl and mostly kept to herself. She was not close with her sisters or her mother. She had low self-esteem, that was until Trevor came into her life. He taught her how to be sexy and sensual. He bought things out of her that she did not even know existed.

Dara was a fast learner and always eager to please. She was very submissive to Trevor. Dara liked Trevor to be in control while she enjoyed the ride. She wanted to do all kinds of bad things with him. Her passion for Trevor was intoxicating. Being desired by Trevor was all she wanted. He gave multiple orgasms and made her squirt. Trevor was so sexy he should have come with a warning label. Trevor had a great sense of humor and always made her laugh. He was strong, intelligent, and driven. He had a great smile, a good heart and made her feel safe. He made her have confidence in herself. She felt desire, sexy, attractive.

RED'S DEVIL'S

Dara secretly had a dirty mind and a very sensual imagination. Trevor loved everything about her and loved her wild side even more than what was his favorite part of her. The only problem was…Trevor was a married man. Trevor love making with her was focused and intense. It's crazy how sex takes the least amount of time but causes the most trouble. Trevor did things to her that made her feel well…she could barely describe them with words, but Dara was tired of coming in second! Trevor didn't completely belong to her, and she was tired of sharing, so she decided to end it. Trevor had created a monster. He inspired her to be a very sexy person, now she was about to unleash it on the world. The hottest love has the coldest endings. Trevor was her favorite hello, then became her worst goodbye.

Trevor would not leave his wife, so Dara walked away. Rejection is an opportunity for a selection period, now Dara was out for the picking. We are all born sexual creatures. Dara had to find someone that would always put her first. Sexuality is the highest form of authenticity. Dara was authentic as they came. It was time for Dara to find her place. Take back control of her life. She was determined to use her newfound confidence and get everything she wanted and desired.

Dara heard about Reds Devils. Back in the day stripping had never crossed her mind but now she was up for any challenge. Dara was ready to make some money and Reds would be the perfect place. Dara never danced professionally. Fucking with Trevor, he taught her how to tease and entice him by giving him little private shows but that was about all the experience she had. Dara figured it couldn't be that hard. She was a fast learner so she would watch and learn from the other dancers. The hardest part would be to get Red to accept her into his family.

Dara wanted to be one of the Red Devils. Dara wanted money and power. She wanted to make as many men's fantasies come true as she could, and she wanted to make money doing it. She wanted every man to lust after her, to want and desire her. She was not looking for love. Love has nothing to do with what you are expecting to get, only with what you are

RED'S DEVIL'S

expected to give and Dara was tired of being the giver. It was time to receive. Dara was ready to show men why storms are named after women. Dara decided it was time to make that change. Her first stop was to Reds Devils.

"Hi, is the manager in? I would like to audition." Dara was nervous and felt butterflies in her stomach. Not just butterflies, but she had the whole zoo in her stomach. She was so nervous she felt like she would throw up." I am Lisa, you can follow me this way." Lisa led her to Red's office. She didn't knock she just walked straight in.

"Someone is here to see you; she wants an audition" Lisa winked at Dara and quietly left the room.

"Well, hello, aren't you a beautiful little creature?" Red smiled and licked his lips.

"I am Dara, it's nice to meet you, and thank you for the compliment." Dara notices Red staring at her.

"Excuse me, you make it hard for me not to stare" Dara felt her face turning red, d she began to blush.

"Sorry it's just that I have a deep desire to know how much your body can take to let the sensations take control of you. To have you exposed and bare so you can feel everything and not resist..."

Dara was speechless. She just stood there blushing. "I want to kiss every corner of your body." Red stood up and walked around from his desk. He stood in front of Dara taking in all her beauty.

"You see Ms. Dara I have a dirty mind and you're on it."

He brushed her long pretty hair behind her ears so he could see her face better in the light. She was even more beautiful. It was time for her audition. Red took Dara by the hand and led her to what looked like a closet or a utility closet door.

"Where are we going?" Dara got a little uneasy.

"I call this my toy box. Have a look around and get comfortable."

Dara could not believe her fucking eyes. There was a stripper pole of course but there was a sex swing hanging from the ceiling. There were whips, chains, handcuffs, and mouth gags. Every kind of dildo, vibrator, and strap-on you could imagine. Nipple clips, anal beads, and lubrication of all kinds.

RED'S DEVIL'S

Different textures and different tastes. Racks of different costumes. A big movie screen on the wall playing porn. Black lights blared down from the ceiling.

It took Dara a moment to take it all in. Is this some type of 50 Shades of grey? Just what exactly was she auditioning for? How many of his girls had auditioned for Red in his toy box? Dara had to pull it together. This is what she wanted…to be desired and wanted. To be irresistible, now was her time to shine. To prove to him and herself that she was in control. No one would ever put her second again. Red wanted an audition then he was going to get one.

Dara went behind the changing wall and picked out a pair of black leather boots with six-inch heels, a black pleated skirt, and a black corset. She put on a collar. Then picked out a leather horse whip and grabbed the blindfold and handcuffs. She did a glance around the room to see if there was anything else for her to play with. She felt well-equipped for the time being. Let the games begin.

RED'S DEVIL'S

Dara was in total control when Red was sure he knew he had made the right decision. She would belong to him and become a part of his handpicked family. Dara slowly began unbuttoning his shirt, removed it from his exquisite body and dropped it on the floor. Dara cracked the whip in the air.
"Take your clothes off. What are you waiting for?
"Whatever you say, darling."

He undid his belt and let his pants fall to the floor. Then he dropped his briefs.
" Socks too Mr. devil."

Dara walked up to him and gave him a long deep kiss while tying the blindfold on his face. Then she pushed him back onto the bed. She kissed his mouth then his neck. Down to his chest, sucking and licking each one of his nipples. She could feel his dick throbbing up and down hard as a rock. She grabbed his balls and squeezed them gently, then harder.
He moaned in pleasure and bit down on his bottom lip. He softly bit her neck. Then he licked and blew in her ears. He sucked her nipples and watched her squirm. He spread her legs and dove in deep. Licking

her clit, kissing her pussy& lips, and sucking her juices out. She moaned in pleasure. Then he flipped her over and smacked her ass with the whip. She cried out for him to give her more. He bit her shoulder and kissed her back; went down to her ass and spread her cheeks and licked up and down. He kissed each cheek and then smacked it again with the whip.

Dara flipped over and threw her legs on his shoulders. Red was beyond hard and slid his two fingers in to feel her moistness. She was ready and willing. Red finally slid the dick in and Dara immediately exploded all over him. He stroked in and out fast, then he slowed down and then fast again. Dara squeezed her breasts. Her nipples were hard.

He sucked and licked her titties still pounding in her wet pussy. She was so wet that the sheets were splashing. They flipped over and she was on top. She rode Red's big dick back and forth and up and down squeezing his dick with her pussy and pulling on the head then sliding down slowly. Red finally pulled the blindfold off. He pushed Dara backward and exploded all over her stomach. Then slid right back into the pussy.

By now Dara's head was hanging off the bed with her legs around Red's neck. She couldn't take anymore; she kept cuming again and again. Red pulled her up and started teasing her nipples with his tongue. They were grinding against one another in the heated frenzy. They came together and collapsed on the bed panting like they were having an asthma attack at the same time. Dara was now a devil. They both calmed down and got themselves together and left the toy box. They were back in Red's office. Red sat behind his big cherry oak desk and pulled out the file. He wrote "Daring Dara" on it then slid it across the desk to her. He had some forms for her to fill out and his list of rules. Dara was reading over the paperwork and thought to herself, was she signing her life away to this man? She read over everything and realized it was basic information.

She signed it and slid back to Red.

"You are officially a devil Daring Dara!" He had a big Kool-Aid smile on his face.

RED'S DEVIL'S

"So now what?' Dara asked.

"Now you begin your new life with lots of fucking money."

Red opened the drawer in his desk and pulled out a stack of $100 bills. He did not even count them; he just handed them to Dara.

"This is to get you ready."

"Go do some shopping get everything you need and be here tomorrow at 4 PM."

"Wow!" "Ok, I guess I will see you tomorrow." Dara put the money in her bra. Then she stood up and shook Red's hand. Red kissed Dara on her forehead and then on her nose. He gave her titties a nice firm squeeze.

"I'm not done with you Daring Dara". Red had plans for her.

"Why do you keep calling me Daring Dara?" Dara asked Red.

"Because most women would not dare just show up to my club unannounced asking for a job. I handpicked all these women. You are the first to ever get hired like this." Dara was surprised by that.

RED'S DEVIL'S

"Did they all audition in the toy box?" she was more than curious.

"That's not up for discussion my beautiful Daring Dara." Red walked her to the door.

"Lisa will help you with the shopping, she knows exactly what you will be needing. I take it, you have transportation?" Red asks his lovely new devil.

"Yes, it gets me from point A to point B. I made it here thankfully." Dara had a car, it was not that dependable, but it did its job until she could afford something better. "Well, we will take care of that tomorrow my love." Dara did not know what that meant, she would have to wait until tomorrow to see just what that meant for her but for now, she had to find Lisa and go shopping!

Chapter 4

LISA

Lisa was born in Fairmont, WV along with nine other siblings. She was blessed to have both parents living. Unfortunately, two of her brothers were incarcerated fighting a murder charge. Lisa was a beautiful, brown-skinned diva. She was about 6 feet tall, she weighed 185 pounds, and her breasts were a 36C cup with a fat ass and thick hips and thick thighs.

Lisa met Red when she was 15 years old and has been with him ever since. Lisa practically ran Red Devil and all his devils listened to Lisa. She was like his enforcer. She was also his top moneymaker. Red had the utmost respect for Lisa in every way. He also had a huge sexual appetite for Lisa. He could never get enough of her.

Lisa was raised by a strong queen. She had a good strong support system in her family and Lisa did not go down the wrong path. She made her path and took it. Lisa knew at an early age that she was her own person. She wanted to play by her own rules. She grew into her sexuality at a young age. Lisa was ready to turn her fantasies into reality which is how she ended up being Red's number one.

Lisa had no plans to go anywhere, anytime soon. They were a power team. Dirty minds think alike. She knows we all are searching for someone whose demons play well with ours period.

Lisa became addicted to Red because he had a good heart and a dirty mind period. He would kiss her as if she were the only thing keeping him alive. Although Lisa was only 15 years old when they met, she had stolen Red's heart. She promised Red if he kept her safe, she would keep him wild.

It was like Red had Lisa in training from the age of 15 until she was 18 years old period. Red did everything to her body imaginable and unimaginable, except fuck her. Those were some of the most intense years of her life. Lisa plays by her own rules, but she plays by his as well. Red is a very patient man. Lisa belonged to him and when he finally had her, she would be the perfect person. Lisa became the embodiment of sexuality and sensuality. Red was

RED'S DEVIL'S

fascinated, obsessed, and infatuated with Lisa all at the same time.

In those four years, Red taught Lisa everything about the real estate business and running Red Devil. By the age of 21 Lisa owned property and had a healthy 401K. She was living her best life. Lisa knew she was not the only woman in Red's life. He had his devils and his auditions. There was a silent understanding between the two of them. Even though Red had an insatiable hunger for Lisa, she saw the best in him and the worst in him and chose both. Red taught Lisa to push her boundaries, explore her limitations and discover what stimulated her. Lisa wanted to be irresistible and wanted by all men. There was one rule Red had for Lisa, something he reminded her of quite a lot. He told Lisa it might be between her legs, but he owned it. Red did not have to look for a perfect lover, he created one, period.

Lisa's confidence was one of her sexiest traits. Every freaking girl needed a gentleman, and every gentleman needed a crazy bitch by his side to hold him down. Lisa was the girl that made Red risk everything. Red knew from the beginning Lisa was a bad idea, but he loved bad ideas with the right person. There was no such thing as inappropriate behavior. As the years went by, they made more money together, building an empire together. King and queen sitting on their throne, at least that's how Lisa pictured it in her head. It is hard to resist a bad guy who is a good man. She wanted a man to hold her hand and pull her hair. Red was what Lisa wanted, he knew how to give it to her and gave it to her every time. He had not let her down yet. Now that Lisa was older, she started following Red's rules less and less. She did what she wanted, not caring if he would approve or not. Lisa knew Red would never ban her from the family. Lisa was there to stay. Lisa was the only woman Red would never get tired of loving. Red could not imagine Lisa not being by his side. His imagination always carried him back to Lisa. Red surprised Lisa by taking Dara into the toy box. He had never interviewed anyone like that since Naomi.

What was so special about Dara? Lisa would sit back later, observe for a while and put some things

RED'S DEVIL'S

together but for now, she would be the perfect hostess period. Time to take Dara shopping and get the new devil ready to make that money. Lisa hoped Dara was cut out for this lifestyle and was willing to follow all the rules that were the only way she would survive at the Red Devil.

"I guess it is time to get you started, I will have you all ready for your big day tomorrow." "Are you sure you are ready for this?" "It's a tough industry with lots of competition to be the top dancer."

Lisa was looking at Dara trying to figure her out

"I see all these women are beautiful, and their bodies are amazing! I do not look like that. I don't even have an ass! What was I thinking?" Dara was getting a little worried. These women were professionals and sexy as hell. Dara knew she was going to have to step her game up.

"Sexy is not always about ass and titties. It's about the way you talk and the way you walk."

"Confidence is what makes you sexy, elegance and smartness is the sexiest thing a woman can have"

RED'S DEVIL'S

Lisa was trying to reassure Dara that she had made the right decision and that she would be simply fine. The first time is always the scariest.

Lisa thought back to her first time on stage, she was so damn nervous! She was rocking her favorite red stilettos and this sexy-ass red lace bodysuit with the crouch out. Red was Lisa's favorite color because she looked so good in it. Red set off well with her beauty.

In the first song, you would have to come on in your costume, in the second song you had to go topless and in the last song you were completely nude.

When she stepped on the stage, she saw lots of men in the crowd, and they were there to see and tip her. She was their fantasy. It was Lisa's job to find out what they wanted and to do it a lot. Lisa was more than just a girl with wet dreams and some sticky fingers, she was a woman taking whatever she needed thanks to these rich successful men donating to her exceptionally large bank account. Lisa was a pro at getting money out of them without having to work hard. Now she would have to teach Dara the tricks of

the trade. "I don't have to fuck these guys, do I? Because I am not trying to go that route I just wanted to dance and make some good money." I'm working on bettering my life and changing my situation." Dara had newfound confidence, but she still was not sure. "Do you have a man or a woman?" Lisa asks Dara.
"Not now, I recently broke it off with someone."
Dara still thought about Trevor. It was much too late now. Things were going to change for the better. Dara did not need Trevor to make her feel good anymore. She did not need Trevor for anything ever again. There was no backing out now. She knew she could do it. Like Lisa said, the first time is always the scariest. Besides if she could fuck a man, she only knew for seven minutes she could seduce and entice the men at the club. Dara was ready, she told herself everything would be all right.

"You don't have to do anything you don't want to do."
"You decide what you will and will not do. Long as you don't break the second rule, no drugs of any kind."

RED'S DEVIL'S

Lisa pulled out a blunt and a bag of weed. She broke the blunt down, emptied the shell, and rolled up.
"I thought you just said no drugs of any kind!" Dara was confused."
"Do as I say not as I do, and you will be just fine." Lisa winked and lit the blunt.
"I don't smoke weed anyway, just cigarettes and some Hennessy is good for me." Dara tried weed once before, but she didn't care for it. She was drug-free.
"Don't worry about me, I'm a big girl, I can manage Red."
Lisa knew her smoking weed did not matter; she had Red wrapped around those sexy long legs. She did what she damn pleased.
"Well, you do not have to worry I won't say anything to Red" Dara thought it was none of her business.
"I'm not worried you can tell him or not, either way, I'm not worried" Lisa laughed and hit her blunt again while Dara lit a cigarette.
They pulled up to a double-wide trailer where an old white couple lived and sold dance clothes there. It had wall-to-wall costumes, boots, stilettos, and toys. Lisa

RED'S DEVIL'S

went through the trailer picking out costumes when she thought they would enhance Dara's beauty. It did not take Lisa long at all, she was a pro. Dara could tell Lisa had been doing this for a while. As they were paying for everything and leaving, Britney walked into the trailer.

Chapter 5

BRITTANY

Brittany was also born and raised in Fairmont WV. She was raised by her mother. She had a relationship with her dad until he passed away a few years ago. She had four brothers and sisters. She did not go anywhere without her dog Storm. They used to ride around in her little Kia together all the time. Brittany has been hustling since she was 15 years old, and she kept a fat blunt rolled always. She did about six months on a weed charge and got probation. Now she was riding around in her Lexus and making more money than she imagined.

Brittany and her best friend Asia were balling out of control. Life was good for Brittany, but she wanted more. She wanted money but most of all, a good man. It would not be hard for Brittany to get a good man because she was beautiful and she knew it.

She was 5 feet three inches, weighed 120 pounds, had breast cup pressed, and had Hazel eyes with a gorgeous face. Her gold and diamonds looked good on her skin. She loved jewelry; she had a couple of tattoos but no piercings. She had a diamond that meant everything in the world to her. It was a diamond heart ring she wore around her neck on a gold necklace. It was a gift from the only man she thought she would ever love. He was now gone, murdered in front of the local liquor store for his jewelry. His name was Andrew, and he was taken too damn soon. He took her heart with him and left her with a diamond heart to remember him by period. Now love was off the table and it was only a romantic thought in her mind. She wanted a man that would break her bed, not her heart.

Brittany wanted to capture Andrew's face the last time she saw it and freeze it forever. Andrews love for Brittany went down to her bones, deeper than anything she ever experienced. He loved her as if someone was working 24 hours to take her from him. He always bent her over and made her feel some type of way. He tasted like everything she always wanted. She could still remember how good his tongue felt down there. His face looked so much better between her legs and an orgasm a day usually kept the doctor away. Now it was all over, no more lovemaking with Andrew. He was the taste in her mouth she would always desire. Now it was just her and her dog Storm against the world. That is how Brittany met Red.

She was at the adult toy store looking for something to help her out for the time being. Even though nothing could replace Andrew, Red was there picking up a package.

"Are you in line, miss pretty" Red asked Britney while looking her over?"

"No Sir." She kept browsing through the store.

"Could I ask you your name?" Red found Brittany very alluring.

"I am Brittany." She was not paying him any attention.

"I see you are a remarkably busy woman. Would it be possible to give you my business card?" Red pulled a card out of his wallet.

"I'm Red, I own the strip club Red Devil would you be interested in working for me?"

RED'S DEVIL'S

Britney had never stripped before unless you count the shows she used to do for Andrew. Stripping never crossed her mind; she was hustling and taking care of herself. Of course she heard about Red, but he never got her attention. She was her own boss. She played by her own rules. No one would ever control her. She gave herself completely to Andrew and she lost him. Her soul wasn't built to take another loss.

Red was a very persistent man.

"I never thought about it, it's not my thing, maybe I could come by and check your place out and see what I can see."

Red smiled to himself. He had a feeling Brittany would like everything she saw.

"I promise you it will be to your liking, just come down tonight and check it out, then we can talk."

Red shook Brittany's hand and walked out of the store with his package.

He may have just found himself a new devil. He was confident that he would be able to impress Britney. Only the most exotic women in the state could be a devil. Red Hat has some digging to do. He had big plans for Brittany. He would convince Britney to become a devil. He would show her just how good she would have it. Stripping may never cross Britney's mind but Red would open her eyes so she could see just how good she would have it.

Brittany was curious to see just what Red had to offer. She would see it becoming a devil was all that it was cracked up to be. Brittany was a freak, but she was more of a private freak. She did not display it publicly she was more of a low-key type. Brittany did what she did with a selected few and the money was great. Brittany thought about what if the rumors were true, was she ready for this? Was Red as ruthless as people said he was? People in Fairmont talk shit all the time so you could never believe people around here. They are quick to make shit up.

Britney did not like people so if she fucked with you, she fucked with you hard. Brittany had a stank-ass attitude. Meeting her for the first time you would think she was a total bitch. Brittney did not care if you or the next bitch liked her or not. She stayed in her lane. She did not mind riding solo. As long as she had Storm and her strap, she was good. Nobody has caught her slipping yet. She has been in plenty of club and bar fights. She could manage herself finely.

Brittany knew Red had rules, but she had rules of her own as well. They would have to come to an understanding if she even decided to try him. Did she want to deal with all the bitches all day and night? Her patience ran thin. She didn't want to talk and she didn't need any new friends. She was going to have to let these hoes know off the rip. She is not about to be braiding her hair and drinking wine. She ain't on that shit. The only bitch she fucked with was her best friend, Asia. She would check Red Devil and then decide if she wanted to deal with all these different people. Red might not want to put up with her short evil ass.

Brittany smiled and thought about what Andrew would think if he was still here. Red would not even be a thought in her mind. Brittany tried not to think about Andrew. It was too painful, with too many memories that brought up too many emotions.

RED'S DEVIL'S

She focused on what she was about to do tonight at Red Devil. Would she secure her bag or walk away? If Red had his way, she would be a devil, then she would be his….

Chapter 6

RED'S DEVIL'S

RED DEVIL

Red went into his office and picked up the phone. He dialed the only police officer on his payroll. Detective Yields, Red needed him to run a license plate and get a background on one of his potential devils. Detective Yields like to dabble in the dark side of S&M. He was a freak through and through. He had an excessively big sexual appetite. Red quenched Yield's sexual appetite and detective Yields kept Red up on any activity about or around his business.

Red and Yields go back a long way. They were in the same foster home and became best friends over the years. They have been scratching each other's back ever since. Red needed to find out more about Brittany and Amber. There was no way that Red would let Amber just walk away. He was used to getting what he wanted. He wanted Amber. He was hoping Britney wouldn't play hard to get because she was hard to forget.

RED'S DEVIL'S

Red was determined to have Amber as his own. Her turning him down just added fuel to his fire. He would not give up on that conquest. For now, he had to make sure Britney was impressed with what he had to offer. There is no way she would turn down what he had to offer her. Red had a way of convincing people to do what he wanted. Everything and everybody had a price. Red was willing to pay. There was no way Red was going to let Amber slip away.

TRAILOR

"Excuse me, I'm looking for something to audition in." Brittany said to the old man."

"Do you have a favorite color?" The old man asked Brittany

"No, not really." Britney knew what she looked good in, and it did not have to be a particular color. Lisa couldn't help but overhear Brittany saying she was going to audition somewhere.

RED'S DEVIL'S

"Did you say you were auditioning, sorry not trying to be in your business or anything? It's just that I represent Red Devil and you would fit in with the rest of the girls perfectly."

Lisa walked over to Brittany with this sexy red two-piece outfit with some stiletto red and silver.

"This should fit you perfectly. I think these shoes should be your size." Lisa handed the outfit and heels to Brittany.

"Wow you are good; these are exactly my size. You work here?"

"No, but I'm here a lot." Lisa laughed.

"I am not sure about auditioning. I was just going to check it out, but I decided to grab something just in case." Britney was holding the red two-piece up to see how it would look on her and the outfit was sexy as hell. "Bring this with you just in case you decide to try us." "You're going to need some garter belts as well." Lisa picked up a few garter belts and handed them to Brittany. "I just got hired there myself, I am Dara, nice to meet you." Dara shook Britney's hand. "I am Lisa." Lisa shook Britney's hand as well.

RED'S DEVIL'S

"I believe I met your boss Red, earlier at the toy store."

"Yes, that was him, a sexy white man that looked like money. I am surprised he let you get away." Lisa knew Red's taste. Brittany fell into Red's category of beautiful and exotic.

Britney got right down to business. "I am not a friendly person, no disrespect to anyone but I like my peace and my privacy. I do not hang out with a lot of females. So, I might not work well with others. I am just being real. I know I have a funky disposition when it comes to bitches." Lisa saw Britney was a feisty one and thought no wonder Red had his eye on her. She will certainly bring in a lot of business." Lisa wondered if Brittany would be auditioning in the toy box with Red.

It did not matter to Dara, it's not like she was jealous or anything, just curious. She wanted to know more about her mysterious, freaky boss Red or, as she liked to call him Mr. Devil. Lisa assured the 2 new devils, "Don't worry you two, whatever doors that come to us, we will open together. I will be there to make sure you are comfortable and Red always keeps us safe." "Anything you need you can ask me. If you have any trouble with any of the girls let me know and I will take care of it for you. As long as you follow the rules you should be just fine,"

"Red will go over all you need to know when he sees you. It is nothing to worry about. It is a bunch of rich horny, lonely, divorced, retired freaky men at the Red Devil."

"They come to play, and they pay as they play." Red would be incredibly happy if Lisa could get Brittany to become a devil. Brittany was a little rougher around the edges than Dara was. She would have to put in some one-on-one time with Brittany. None of the Red devils intimidated Lisa. No one was competing for her. She was the shit, which is all it was to it. She did her job very well.

"Will we be seeing you tonight?" Lisa asks Brittany while picking out more outfits for Dara.

"I am thinking about it, I haven't decided yet." Brittany was looking at some more costumes.

RED'S DEVIL'S

"Well, this is from Mr. Red, so if you don't like it, you will not have wasted your money." Lisa paid the old man for Britney's outfit and stilettos.

"Hope to see you soon Brittany." Lisa handed Brittany her bag and Brittany left. She had to go smoke her blunt and decide on what to do.

Lisa and Dara continue to shop; they spent about $1500 on costumes for Dara. Lisa had her all the way ready. Dara was still nervous, but she was also a little excited at the same time. Today was going to be the first day of the rest of her life. A life she would live on her terms.

Lisa seemed cool and all to Dara, she just was not trying to get so close to anyone. She did know one thing about strippers, they are competitive and can be cutthroat. Dara thought Brittany would be able to handle herself. Dara was a lover, not a fighter. If it came down to it Dara would fight, she just was never really in any such situation where she had too before. At least not since she was younger and fighting with her sisters. Fighting was the least of Dara's worries. No fighting was one of Red's rules. No physical violence, no verbal abuse, and no drugs. That was all fine by Dara.

"I know you read over the rules, there is one rule that's not in the paperwork." Lisa told Dara.

Lisa pulled her shirt over her shoulder and revealed to Dara a red tattoo of some devil horns. It was a small simple tattoo, but it was still a tattoo that was permanent. Dara did not know she was going to have to be branded for life! What if she didn't like working at Red Devil? Then she would have this permanent tattoo on her body for the rest of her life!" Wow, a tattoo, it seems more like a brand. I have tattoos but they all have a meaning. Dara was not too sure.

Lisa said, "It's not that serious just showing your loyalty to the family." Dara figured it would not be hard to cover something so small.

"I could always get it covered up. It's so small"

"I don't think you will have a reason to get it covered. It is not like being branded like an animal. Just so you know you have a family for the rest of your life, money, and protection as well."

RED'S DEVIL'S

Dara thought it all sounded good, it just seemed like Red was trying to own her instead of managing her. Dara tried to prepare herself for what was to come. All she could do was pray for the best. Lisa made it sound so simple. That probably was part of the job to convince girls to become devils. Dara wondered how many times Lisa had done this exact thing and how many of them fell for it?

Red had 15 girls in the Red Devil. Each one was a different size, shape, and race. He had a variety of beauty to highlight. The club was very elegant. There were two bars, a kitchen, and a public restroom. The dancers had a bathroom, and a shower and their dressing rooms were huge. It had two poles on stage, and they were chandeliers hanging from the ceilings. He had a dining area to eat in, leather furniture, and on the main floor, everything was cherry oak and mahogany. The private rooms were upstairs. He had three jacuzzi rooms on the third level. There was security at both entrances and exits. Security in the parking lot and of course two bouncers at the main entrance. The guys were not allowed to touch you

RED'S DEVIL'S

while you were on stage dancing. Every drink you sold, you made money off of it and you kept all your tips. Even the jacuzzi room was $500 for two hours with a bottle of expensive champagne. The girls were always dressed on the floor. There was no smoking in the club at all, not even vaping was allowed. The dancers had to play their songs on a jukebox. The walls were painted black, and all the costumes glowed under the black light. You could never tell what time it was inside Red Devil. There were mirrors all over the club. The place was amazing, and the atmosphere was very inviting.

Dara had never seen a strip club that looked like Red Devil. It was truly one of a kind. Lisa had to make sure Dara was ready for tomorrow and get things ready for Brittany tonight. Lisa didn't know anything about Amber yet. That was a conquest Red would overcome himself. He liked a good challenge and he also liked to win. Red always came in the first place. He never settled for a second. Amber did not know who Red was, but she was about to find out exactly who he was and what he could and would do to be the winner. He was going to win Amber over if it was the last thing he did. All he needed was a little information so he could know which move to make. Detective Yields always came through for Red. If and when any of his devils were in some trouble which they rarely would, Detective Yields would make their problems go away. It was always something like parking tickets, stalkers, or an angry ex-boyfriend, nothing major. Red ran a tight ship. They were to always conduct themselves as ladies in and outside the club. Red kept a close eye on all his devils. He had a reputation to uphold. His girls represented him. Being as close to perfect as they can is already expected from them. His devils had it made, and they knew it.

Chapter 7

RED'S DEVIL'S

DETECTIVE YIELDS

Detective Yields worked for the Fairmont police. He was six feet 2 inches tall with red curly hair and a red beard and mustache. He had green eyes and weighed about 180 pounds. A Good-looking white boy. He was born in Morgantown WV and was in foster care with Red, that is how they became best friends. They played on the same basketball team together in high school and they even went to West Virginia University where Red went into business and real estate while Yields studied criminal justice before going to the Academy. He came from a long line of cops. From his great-grandfather down to his dad, and all his uncles.

Yields and Red were like brothers; they were remarkably close. Their bond became even stronger as they got older. Detective Yields moved up the ranks pretty early in his career. He had the best-solved case record in West Virginia. He was incredibly good at what he did. After graduating at the top of his class period, he thought about joining the FBI in Virginia. Then he would be big shit. Yields were a very driven man; he demanded results and he got them. That is why he was such a good friend to Red. They both enjoyed the power and just like Red, Yields was a bachelor. He loved women too much to settle down with just one. He could have a different woman whenever he wanted. Another thing he had in common with Red was that his sexual appetite was enormous. Since he rarely sought it, his best friend made sure that his needs were met. Yields frequented Red Devil every chance he got. Red Devil was like his second home, and he was living very well. Yields lived in an impressively large and nice property that Red had given him. He had money and he was a very generous man. When it came to his sexual escapades, he had his favorite girls. What would you call his regulars? They knew just what he wanted and just how to give it to him. He was a very satisfied customer. They made sure that all of his deepest, darkest fantasies come true over and over again.

Now Yields had some digging to do for Red. Yields had done this for him so many times before he knew what Red would want him to find out. He gathered as much info on Amber as he could. It was not much because she did not have a record. Yields would have to do a little footwork.

DARA

Dara was thinking about Red and what he said about her car that they would take care of that tomorrow. Lisa's fire engine red Rolls- Royce was outstanding! Dara wondered how much that set Lisa back or did Red take care of that for Lisa like he said he would do for her tomorrow? How long do you have to dance to get a ride like that? Dara did not know what to think. She was trying to take it all in. Was this actually about to be her new reality? Fancy cars, fancy clothes, and a boatload of money? Who would be dumb enough to turn that down? To turn Red down? Big things were happening for Dara in a short amount of time, could it get any better? Dara smiled to herself; it was not so bad being a devil after all.

RED'S DEVIL'S

Dara figured it was time to get home and get some rest so she would be ready for tomorrow. Her first day as a red devil and she was feeling nervous and anxious. Dara did not think she would get much sleep; she had entirely too much on her mind to sleep. She finally fell asleep thinking about what her family would say and realized that she did not give a care in the world. Their opinion meant nothing to Dara. She stopped caring a long time ago. She did not have to prove herself to her family or anyone else. This was her life and she intended on living it to the fullest. No time for regrets, she had already signed her name on the dotted line.

AMBER

Amber did not know what to make of Red. He was very pushy, and she felt like he had an attitude toward her for turning him down. She did not give a fuck. Amber was not about to become a devil and start stripping! She did not work for tips, and she never would. That was a chump change for her. She liked the big paydays, no time for playing with these grown men for a few dollars. She was already in the big league. Red would have to find someone else to be his devil. She did not give it a second thought.

She had some money to make on her terms. She took her bag of tricks and headed home. Time to check her schedule. Someone would be wanting Lola's services. Lola was Amber's alter ego. Lola was in high demand. Her clients could not get enough of Lola, she was every man's dream come true.

Chapter 8

FRED

Fred was born in Fairmont, West Virginia. He was 50 years old and weighed 280 pounds; 5 foot 9 inches tall and was all muscle. Fred had dark skin and brown eyes with a low military haircut. You would see him in his army fatigues all the time he was in the Marine Corp. for over 30 years. Fred was an only child raised by both parents. When he was younger Fred, his mom and grandmother were exceptionally close friends until his grandmother passed away.

Fred was a very serious man but a big teddy bear deep down. Fred had been with Red since the beginning and 15 years later, he was still there. Red kept Fred around because he was good at his job, damn good! Fred took care of every one of the Red Devils. He took his job very seriously. He was the protector. Fred made sure nothing went down at the Red Devil that was not supposed to.

Red depended on Fred to take care of his devils and Fred had not disappointed him yet. He had a remarkably close relationship with Lisa. He treated her as if she was his daughter. He had known Lisa since the first day Red brought her to the Red Devil. She was only 15 years old then, a little girl. Now she was a full-grown woman. Fred still treated her like she was that young 15-year-old girl. He would kill anyone that tried to hurt her, and he did not care who it was even if that someone was Red...

RED'S DEVIL'S

LISA (RED DEVIL)

Lisa dropped Dara off and drove back to the Red Devil.

"Here baby girl let me get those bags. You know better. What if you chipped or broke a nail? What if you tripped in your heels carrying all of these bags? Now hand them over!" Fred took the bags from Lisa. Lisa gave up the bags and said, "I've been walking in these heels for 15 years and I'm a big girl."

Fred grinned at Lisa saying

"I know, you give me the same speech every time. I know you can manage yourself but when I am here, it's my job and my honor to look out for you."

"I know, you give me the same speech as well. I love you teddy Freddie."

That was Lisa's nickname for Fred. He was a big life-size teddy bear. She loved Fred just as much as he loved her. He was like a father figure to Lisa. She let Fred carry her bags in for her. She put all the costumes and dresses that she bought for Dara and put them in her locker in the dressing room. Then she headed to Red's office.

RED'S DEVIL'S

"I ran into one of your potential devils today." She sat down in the big, oversized leather chair across from Red's desk "Amber?" Red leaned up in his chair with a big grin on his face.

"Amber? "No, who is Amber?"

"I meant Britney. She was deciding whether or not she wanted to become a devil and Dara ran into her at the trailer. I could tell she was more than a little curious. I could see the wheels in her head spinning."

"Well, that is good to hear. Make sure the devils are on their best behavior." Lisa smiled.

"I like you better with a smile and no clothes on." Red smiled and licked his lips.

"If you could read my thoughts right now you would be traumatized and turned on all at the same time." Lisa told Red laughing to herself.

"Do what the voices in your panties tell you to do." Red said to Lisa laughing with her.

"If I wanted any lip from you, I would sit on your face." Red stuck his tongue out at her. A man that knows how to use his tongue is extremely useful. Lisa walked out of his office but before Lisa could close the door, Red said, "I've been thinking long and hard about what I'm going to do to you tonight." Lisa waved him off and closed the door. Red still had not figured out how to sit across from Lisa and not be turned on. Time to turn on the charm. Brittany should be arriving soon, and Red was more than ready.

Chapter 9

BRITTANY

Brittany was not sure if she wanted to do this, she didn't know how to feel about the whole situation. All she could do was show up and see if his spot was popping like he said it would be. It was Friday, so hopefully, it would be a good crowd. She could not believe she was going to do this. What was she thinking? She needed this chance for a change.

Brittany loved the idea of making a boatload of money. She just wasn't sure if she was built for stripping physically or mentally. Brittany wasn't really into wearing fancy dress, she was more of a jeans and gym shoe type of girl pulling her hair back in a ponytail and calling it a day. She wasn't about to switch up now just to go to a strip club, she wasn't trying to impress anyone. Red was trying to impress her. Brittany was as ready as she could be. She talked herself into just showing up to take it from there and she would see if she could fall for Red charm and become a devil, or would she stick to what she knows best, making her own money under her terms. Besides, she had a good plug on the work tip. She always has top-notch products. Her people loved her quality and her quantity. She did not need a middleman to help make money. Brittany was doing fine on her own. Why fix something that is not broken? Is it time for Brittany to change up her scene?

Brittany walked to the door where Fred checked her ID and patted her down for weapons. Then he escorted her to the rest office. Brittany was taking it all in. It was gorgeous inside the Red Devil. It was so much more than she expected. The women were all dressed up in evening gowns and stilettos and a naked chick on stage with all kinds of money laid out for her. The men were enjoying themselves.

"Miss Brittany, so glad you decided to show up." Red was curious to know what was going on in that pretty little head of hers.

"It is impressive I can say that much. It is a pretty nice setup here." Brittany went to light a cigarette.

"Sorry, Miss Brittany, there is no smoking in my office or the entire establishment under any circumstances. Not even in my parking lot. That is one of the few rules we have here at the Red Devil."

Red pulled out a file from his desk and handed it to Brittany, it had her name on it. "This is some forms for basic information as well as a list of my rules, read them over and let me know how you feel about the Red Devil."

Brittany opened the file and began reading over the rules. "I noticed when I walked in that all the women on the floor had evening gowns on what's that about?"

"My girls are classy. My place is classy. They need the proper attire for the atmosphere. The prettiest gowns were meant to be taken off Miss Brittany."

Brittany smiled; Red smiled again then put his hand over his heart

"I'm not really into dresses."

Brittany continued to read the forms in her file. Red was looking at Brittney and watching how she moved.

"The only thing bothering me right now is your clothes." Brittany smiled and said, "You can stop undressing me with your eyes, try using your teeth instead." That took Red by surprise.

"I want to taste you on my fingertips," Red said to Brittany. He stood up and walked over to Brittany.

RED'S DEVIL'S

"Show me where you want me to bite. You know bite marks are like love notes left in the flesh. I think we should do something that makes us both moan, take your clothes off, I have a plan."

"I am sure you do, Mr. Red." Brittany had to laugh, was this guy serious? Red leaned over and kissed Brittany on her neck.

"If you kiss me there, I'm not responsible for what happens next." Brittany gave Red a fair warning.

"I am hungry for your taste b

Bold Brittany!" That would be her name for now because she was very bold. He could tell she was a very blunt and honest person, not afraid to speak her mind.

"We are going to be good at being bad together. I see we will be incredibly good for one another."

Red knew he made the right choice from the moment he laid eyes on Brittany.

"I'm not trying to be sexy, it's just my way of expressing myself when I move around." Brittany explained to Red. "May I kiss you Bold Brittany? A kiss seals two souls forever in time. I am turned on by

RED'S DEVIL'S

every thought of you." Brittany looked at Red trying to figure out what it was about him that tapped into her private, freaky mind. It was as if something was pulling her closer to him. He had this aura around him that made him almost irresistible.

"I'm letting you know that I'm a handful, hope you can manage me, that's why you have two hands."

"Right now, I just want to pin you against the wall and take all of you. There is nothing more artistic than lovemaking." Red was hard as a rock.

He felt this strong urge to be inside Brittany. He loved the way her mind worked. Brittany felt his chemistry, it was as if he touched her, he would set her soul on fire. "You can stay but your clothes must come off."

Red was ready, Brittany's sexiness was driving him insane. He needed her, wanted her. He felt as if he could explode all over her face right now without even being inside of her yet. Brittany teased Red until he was begging for it. "I think about you a little more than I should Bold Brittany. Feel free to shut me up with your kisses." "Then will you be a good boy?"

RED'S DEVIL'S

Brittany smiled at Red. She pulled her T-shirt over her head and let it fall to the floor. Then she took her bra off, stepped out of her sneakers, pulled her pants down, then her panties and now was standing completely naked in front of Red. He thought to himself he loved good girls with dirty minds and that they are keepers. Brittany kissed Red with that all-consuming kiss that means something more than a kiss then she kissed his neck. "When you kiss my neck, I feel euphoria!" Red told Brittany.
He felt like Brittany was just what he had been waiting for.

"I have been worried about all of the difficulties which I can face in life except my addition to Hazel eyes and gorgeous smile." That sort of took her breath away. "Some of the best moments in life are the ones you can't tell anyone about." Brittany said to Red, then grabbed his bulging rock-hard dick.
Red picked Brittany up and sat her on his big cherry oak desk. Brittany let out a little giggle. He sucked her titties and sucked her neck then slid his fingers

inside her to see if she was ready for all he was about to give her.

"I may not have been your first, but I do plan on being your last."

Red pushed Britney down on the desk and began to suck her pussy. Brittany thought it was the best head she had had in a good long time. Red was a professional at eating pussy! He hit that spot and she squirted all in his mouth and on his face.

"I cannot taste my lips. Can you do it for me?" Red asked Brittany.

"I know you like that pussy now fuck me like you love it!" Britney was moaning from the pleasure Red was giving her with his tongue.

Red pulled her ass to the edge of the desk knocking shit over without a care. Then he slid his dick in her pussy, it was like fucking waterfall. Brittany wrapped her legs around his neck and began to roll her hips and grind against him and his hard dick.

"Choke me and tell me I am pretty with your dick in my mouth!" Brittany was on the verge of having one hell of an orgasm.

RED'S DEVIL'S

Brittany pushed Red into his oversized leather chair, then squeezed his balls while teasing the top of his dick with her tongue, then slowly taking him in her mouth.

"I love making you work hard."

Brittany looked up at Red, his eyes were rolling in the back of his head. Brittany sucked his dick like she was starving! Red never felt so turned on from getting head. No one but Lisa ever gave him that outstanding head. Red bent her over the desk and gave her deep strokes from the back with his hands around her throat. Brittany thought everybody deserves someone that makes them look forward to their next orgasm. Sex is just not as hot without biting, scratching, and spanking! Red thought about pining her to the wall because she was truly a masterpiece.

Brittany knew good girls go to heaven, but bad girls make you feel like you are in heaven and right now, Brittany was being unbelievably bad with Red. Brittany was surprised at herself for reacting to Red the way she did. Brittany had never done anything like this before. Especially with the white guy she barely knew. What was she thinking!? It was too late now. She had Red hook, line and sinker. Red came all over Brittany's thighs, stomach, and breasts then they were both sticky and sweaty, so he decided to show Brittany his toy box. He usually did his auditions in his toy box, but he could not resist Brittany. She was too damn good at it for some reason.

Brittany could not believe her eyes. What in the world did he have going on up in here? She was thinking he was a freak on a new level of freakiness. Red was some kind of freak; the proof was all around her. Toys she had never seen before. She was amazed by what she saw. They went to take a shower together. Red pinned Brittany to the shower wall and took her from behind until she screamed out in pleasure, their bodies were not the only thing wet at this point. They got dressed and went back into his office.

"Don't worry Bold Brittany, we will have plenty of time to play. When I am good, I'm good... but when I'm bad, I'm much better." Red watched Brittany getting dressed. He could not help but stare at such beauty and such a small package.

Lisa walked into Red's office and saw the mess on the floor of his desk. She was not feeling that situation at all. Red was getting beside himself; he was going too far. She was used to him and other women but lately he has been doing too much. Red was being very extra; she began to look at him differently. Lisa was ready to play if that's what Red wanted to do. He was used to winning all the time. Lisa was about to show him that he could not always have his cake and eat it too. Time to put him on a good pussy diet. Let him know who the fuck is in charge around this bitch. Time for a change. He might not likely say new rules. He gave her all the freedom she wanted and looked past her breaking every one of his rules plus some.

"So how was your audition, Brittany?" Lisa had this cold stare looking at Britney.

"It was very wet." Britney laughed and walked out of Red's office without saying another word to either of them.

RED'S DEVIL'S

"What the fuck was that about?" Red asked Lisa.

"What would you be referring to?" She rolled her eyes and left his office.

She slammed the door so hard that it popped back open. Time to show Red who was really in control.

No more putting up with his shit. She had enough money to secure her future and get the hell out of dodge. Her time was up at the Red Devil. No more being his little errand girl and putting up with his sexual escapades. Lisa had had enough, and she was at her breaking point. She had money, came across property and she was above average that could have any man or woman she wanted. There was just one thing Lisa was missing, her daughter...

Chapter 10

DARA

Dara knew she was not going to get much sleep. She could not stop thinking about Red and the things he did to her body. What did he have that she found so irresistible? Dara could not believe her behavior. What came over her? It was like he put her in a trance or hypnotized her in some kind of way. Dara never behaved like that a day in her life. It was like he knew her secret fantasies, as if he read her mind. She knows that was a ridiculous idea. Still, there was something about Mr. Devil that intrigued Dara. She found Red fascinating.

Dara felt she should eat something, but she was too nervous. The anxiety of becoming a red devil made her feel like she was going to vomit. So instead of worrying and making herself more nervous, she hopped in the shower and shaved. She then got dressed and ready to hit Red Devil. Time to see if she had what it takes to be a devil. There is no backing down now, she could do this. It will not be any harder than her audition, which is for sure the most pleasurable thing in her life. This should be a piece of cake as long as she could find the beat and go from there…

AMBER

Amber thought she was tripping or just high as hell she could have sworn this guy was following her. This is the third time she has seen him while she was out. You cannot miss the red hair. Who was this guy? And why was he following her? She wondered if he was some sort of creepy murderer or stalker. Amber knew he was not one of her clients, that she knew for sure. What the fuck was his problem? She was trying to decide if she wanted to confront him or not. Good thing she was always strapped just in case.

RED'S DEVIL'S

Before Amber could do anything, the redheaded man approached her. Amber put her hand inside her purse to feel the weight of her 32. It always made her feel safe.

"Excuse me, Amber, right?" Yields stuck his hand out.

Amber ignored the gesture and looked Yields up and down.

"Why do you ask, and why do you want to know?" Yields was still holding his hand out. "I am here on behalf of my acquaintance, who really would like to meet with you."

Amber looked at Yields, she had no clue about what he was talking about.

"Are you trying to tell me you have been following me for a friend of yours?" She still held on tight to her gun. "I guess you can say that. He would like you to grace him with your presence. The sooner the better, then I can stop following you all over town." He shrugged his shoulders.

"What if you and your friend are some kinds of perverts following people around?"

RED'S DEVIL'S

Detective Yields smiled, "No ma'am I'm not... we're not some kind of pervert." He kept smiling at Amber. "Who might this acquaintance be?"

Yields took a business card out of his wallet, and it said Red Devils with a devil horn tattoo on it and read the phone number. As soon as Amber read the card, she knew exactly who acquaintance was…Mr. Red. "Listen, tell your perverted friend, that I'm not interested. I told him that already, and no thank you. I am doing simply fine for myself." Amber tried to walk off, but he grabbed her by the arm.

"I do not think that would be a very wise decision, Red does not like to be told no." Amber pulled the 32 out of her purse.

"I told you I'm not interested, now get your fucking hands off me!"

Yields let her arm go. "Calm down Amber, I will let you go for now but trust me you will regret this." Amber hurried to her car and locked her doors. Her heart was racing. She could not believe that Red had her followed. He must have some serious issues. It seemed to her that Red might be a real threat. She was going to have to watch her back. This guy must be crazy. "Who in the hell have people followed? All this to work at a strip bar!" There was no way she was ever going to strip at the Red Devil. "Who does he think he is? What was wrong with him?"

FRED

Fred heard Lisa singing at the bar. He knew when Lisa started singing, she was feeling some type of way. He decided to check on her and make sure she was ok. "What is going on baby girl? I know when you are in your feelings."

Lisa leaned her head on Fred's shoulder. She was too strong to cry, but she could use a hug.
"It's nothing, I cannot handle reality, I'm OK. I just wanted to sing." Fred rubbed her hair.
"We will let it out, baby girl. Remember what I told you about holding so much in? It is not healthy for you physically or mentally." Lisa hugged Fred.
"Don't worry, it is all going to take care of itself. There is always some madness in love but there is also always some reason in madness."

RED'S DEVIL'S

Fred kissed her forehead and gave her a great big hug. "Talk to you later baby girl. Try to enjoy the rest of your day."

Lisa walked off singing to herself. Smiling to herself because she had a big secret. She was about to find out that Red had an even bigger secret...

Chapter 11

BIG PAPA

Big Papa was the chef at Red Devils. He was 40 years old and born in Harlem, New York. He was raised by both his parents along with his seven sisters and four brothers. He graduated high school and did a little college, then he went on to be a chef. Big Papa had three children by three different women. He was engaged to one of his baby mamas until she was brutally murdered. He never really did any serious time, just a few minutes a month in the county. Big Papa started hustling when he was 16 years old. Big Papa lived in Paris for a short time when he was younger. Paris was one of his favorite places to visit. He mostly spent time together with his best friend of over 20 years. They would barhop, drinking bottles of patron and smoking blunts.

Big Papa was a lady lover. He was 5 feet 7 inches tall, 300 pounds with long dreadlocks, and brown eyes. He loved his Nubian Queens, but he also had a taste for Hispanic women too. He was the chef at Red Devil since they opened. His specialty was Caribbean food and soul food. Big Papa enjoyed being in the presence of beautiful naked women. He kept their bellies full, and they kept his dick hard. "Good food and good pussy. Who could ask for anything more?" The money was just as good if not better. He knew every girl's order, and every devil was different. He kept them satisfied. Big Papa enjoyed two things beautiful woman and his beautiful Mercedes 550.

Big Papa had his eye on one devil, in particular, her name was Naomi. Something about that chocolate bunny that Big Papa could not shake. Naomi was a devil for a short period. She was the only one Red let walk away without any repercussions. No one ever knew the whole story about Naomi, she was gone just as fast as she got there. If anyone knew the full story it would be Lisa. She knew any and everything about what went on in the Red Devil. Big Papa could never ask her, but he would sure like to know where she ended up. He hopes she was somewhere safe and happy. What he would not give to see Naomi again. Absence sharpens love and presence strengthens it. If he could choose again, he would still choose her. He would get excited thinking about the things he wanted to do for her.

Big Papa's favorite thing to do is Naomi. Her ability to distract his train of thought is unmatched. He felt like she was the part of him he always needed. Making Naomi smile and making her horny were two of his favorite things. Naomi knew a good man deserved to be deep-throated and Papa was a damn good man. He really missed Naomi and did not think he would ever see her again. No time to think about Naomi; he had food to prepare for his customers. Red depended on Big Papa to serve top-of-the-line meals and Big Papa did just that. His customers never had any complaints. Big Papa had a reputation for being one of the best chefs in West Virginia. He was proud of his work as he should be. Many people have tried to steal Big Papa away from Red, but he stuck with what he knew best. His place was at the Red Devil.

RED

Red was on cloud nine. Two new devils and one potential devil. He had to get ready for his monthly out-of-town trip. Lisa ran Red Devil while he was gone. Red never said exactly where he was going, just that he had business to take care of. Red had a special woman in his life. She was the reason for his out-of-town trips, and he looked forward to them. Red knew if Lisa found out, she would be pissed for sure. He never missed a month in 15 years. Red knew deep down inside that Lisa wanted to know where he was going, but he would never tell her. It would change everything in their relationship. The rear was anxious to see Daring Dara. He could still smell her Burberry perfume. Then he thought about how sweet she tasted. Red liked Dara for her sexiness and courage. He wanted Brittany for her wild side and Amber

RED'S DEVIL'S

would be his prize. Red had to do a few more things before the night was over.

Red sent for Dara. When she arrived at his office he got up and told her to follow him to the parking lot. Fred escorted them outside where there was a green Porsche. "How could she have missed it?" Dara thought. That was her dream car, a Porsche and it was her favorite color green! She let out a little squeal of joy and jumped on Red hugging and kissing him. Red handed Dara the keys and the license plate that said DYRGDARA. There were no words for her, she was so happy. She could not stop smiling.

Red introduced Fred to her, and Fred explained what his job as a security guard consisted of. Dara thought she and Fred would get along simply fine. Fred was an easy-going guy, that was until he had to do his job with the creeps and weirdos. Then the savage came out in him. Fred was perfect for being a bouncer. Dara followed Red back to his office. Before she could sit down, a guy came in with a briefcase. When he opened it up, there was tattoo equipment inside. It was time to get her mark of the devil, little

RED'S DEVIL'S

devil horns on the back of her shoulder. Dara was not afraid of getting a tattoo, she already had a few. What she was afraid of was that it wouldn't work out and she would have the devil horn tattoo on her permanently. Again, she thought about the cover-up. Dara decided to go along with it for now.

Dara noticed Red staring at her "You like what you see Mr. Devil?"

"I'm just admiring the view."

By now the guy is working on her tattoo.

Red said, "I was thinking how good it is to wake up with coffee when I can wake up with you." Dara was turning red from blushing.

"I want you to taste me."

Red says looking deep into Dara's eyes and said, I'm always in the mood to make you cum."

Red had a devilish grin on his face. When the tattoo guy finished, Red pulled out a couple of $100 bills and paid him. When the tattoo guy left Dara walked over to the mirror so she could see her new tattoo. She was officially a devil. Now it was showtime. She

RED'S DEVIL'S

had to get out of his office before Part 2 went down in the toy box. Dara caught Red starting again.

"I love it when I catch you staring at my body, Mr. Devil". Dara licked her lips.

"I want you in my mouth, just not right now. I am in rotation. I have to get ready."

She did not know Red had been ready, all 10 inches of his long hard dick. Red had been ready. He almost did not let her leave. Come on Dara, he was not in a hurry. Now that she belonged to him, he could take his time with Daring Dara. The night was still young; anything is possible at the Red Devil. Tonight, was the night he wanted to push her body to the limits. All Dara could think about was licking, sucking, and slurping on Red. He tasted as if she belonged on her knees.

Chapter 12

DETECTIVE YIELDS

Yields continued to follow Amber, learning as much about her as he could, at least enough to satisfy Red. You did not want to get on Red's bad side or bad things would happen. Even though they were the absolute best of friends, Yields still would not put it past him that Red would make him disappear. Just like all those other people that didn't agree with Red or didn't give him what he wanted. You could be in a world of trouble, and you did not want to be on his bad side, ever. Red gave him a job to do, and he was determined to do it.

Yields followed Amber to EBO's restaurant downtown across the street from the West Banco Bank. He watched her go inside, then got out of his car and walked inside.

RED'S DEVIL'S

"Are you just now ordering fried chicken and greens, straight soul food?" Yields walked into EBO's and saw Amber sitting on the booth and he sat down next to Amber.

"Not you again! I gave you my final answer and told Red to thank you, but no thank you." She was pissed.

"I don't think you understand the importance of this situation." They were both talking low so no one could hear their conversation.

Yields thought Amber was beautiful and he felt some sort of connection to her. She was so damn beautiful he could see why Red was so obsessed with her. It was something about her. He found himself wanting to be near her. To look into her beautiful eyes, to hold her close. Amber had him under her spell with just one look. Amber was not some weak, helpless bitch. Amber knew she would never dance or work with Red, the man was crazy. Detective Yields was infatuated with Amber. Why does Red get to have all the beautiful women? When was he going to be able to choose one that Red has not already touched? He could just tell Red that she had left town, and he couldn't find her. Yields had never betrayed Red in all the 20 years of their friendship, but it was something about Amber that Yields could not explain. The attraction he felt for her was crazy.

"Listen, Amber, just hear me out. I know I kind of creeped you out and yes, I was doing this for Red. The more I see you and the brief moments I've been around you; I feel this need to be close to you. I don't think what Red is doing is ok on any level. He's my best friend and I do things for him even if I don't agree with him. I would love to get to know you better. Trust me, I am not some creepy stalker."

Amber was tripping out. How did he go from stalker to asking her out on a date? Amber had no interest in dating a white guy ever. Yields had his sexy going on, just not sexy enough for Amber to fool with ever. She sat there quietly for a while; she was speechless. Then she thought even if she isn't going to fuck him, she could still keep him close to know what Red was doing. He could be her bodyguard without him even knowing it. They say, "keep your enemy close, and Amber intended to do just that. "Ah, this is weird to me. I know that I am not going to work at Red Devil, and meeting you like this is beyond strange. You seem like a nice enough man Yields, you're just friends with a creep."

"I guess I can let you take me to dinner sometimes. I hope this isn't some scheme to get me to work at the Red Devil because if it is, you are wasting your time. Put your number in my phone and I will call you."

"Trust me, I will manage Red, and you won't have to worry about him. I promise you; I will keep you safe." He put his number in her phone.

"Keep me safe? Is there something you are not telling me? Do I have to worry about this guy? I have heard rumors, but you know how Fairmont talks."

Yields knew that Red was probably still a problem, but he was going to contain the matter. "I will take care of Red, don't worry."

"I am looking forward to your call. We can start over so you will get the perception of me being a creepy stalker or a weirdo out of your head." Amber had to smile a little bit.

RED'S DEVIL'S

"I love it when you do that." Yields told Amber, staring into her eyes.

"Do what?" Amber asked.

"When you smile it is so beautiful, you should do it more often. Together with you is becoming my favorite place."

Amber was used to all kinds of men hitting on her telling her how beautiful she was or how attractive she is. She never had a guy with that approach trying to get with her. It all still seems so strange. Keeping him close with an advantage for Amber. That way she could be one step ahead of Red and know his every move.

"Well, my food is here, so I guess I will talk to you later." Amber got her order and Yields walked her to her car.

"I will be looking forward to your call. Enjoy your food and the rest of your day." Yields opened the door for her and then closed it once she got in. Amber said goodbye and pulled it off. Yields could not believe she agreed to see him, he was extra excited. He felt like a kid on Christmas. He knew

RED'S DEVIL'S

meeting Amber was fate. He could not walk away from what was meant to be. He wondered how he was going to get Red off Amber's radar. Hopefully, he could find some other woman and forget about Amber. If he knew Red like he thought he did, throwing him off Amber's trail was not going to be so easy.

He was fed up with being second and getting the sloppy leftovers. He finally found a girl he could see himself spending the rest of his life with. Yields had to have Amber for himself. Maybe if he just explained the situation to Red, he would let him have Amber all to himself. Yields knows that Red is a womanizer. He treats the devils like they are his property. Yields saw the way Red does Lisa; he has everyone wrapped around his finger. Red was not going to give up that easily. Especially, to let Yields have Amber. To him, she was like a conquest. Red always just got what he wanted by any means necessary. He would take Yields out just as quickly as he would the next guy. Yields had to produce a plan fast. He knew Red would not wait forever. He was going to have to give Red some sort of information about Amber. He had to tell him something.

How could he keep Red away from Amber? How could he be with Amber without Red finding out? What if he could talk Amber into leaving with him as far away from Red as possible? Where they could never be found. He could always transfer his job; he was almost close to being an agent for the FBI. He could go anywhere he wanted without leaving a paper trail. Yields was a very skilled detective; he did not dare to tell Amber that he was a police detective. He would tell her that in time. He did not want to scare her off and miss the chance to be with his soul mate. He learned enough about Amber, that she is so weird. That did not matter to Yields. Once he took her away from this place, she wouldn't need to hustle.

Chapter 13

RED (RED DEVIL)

Red thought it was taking Yields a long time to bring him some information about Amber. He was headed out of town and his patience was thinning each day that Yields said he had nothing.

"This is all you have of her!" Red was upset.

"There's not much to tell. I have followed her for a few days as you said. Just a normal girl hustling weed and getting some clients making a lot of cash."

Red slammed his fist on the desk. "What am I paying you for? I need more than what you bought me! I could have found this shit out from my fucking self for free!" Yields knew he was going to be extremely disappointed. "Did you approach her and talk to her?" Red asked Yields.

"Not yet, I was just learning her routine and all the places she frequents. I can approach her tonight. What exactly am I supposed to say to her?"

RED'S DEVIL'S

Yields was silently debating if he should just come clean and tell Red his feelings are bullshit for Amber. That might put both of their lives in jeopardy. He would have to convince Amber to leave town if he could not change Red's mind about Amber. He had to be with her. She needed to be with him. There had to be a way to keep the effort to himself and have a future with her where they both could stay alive. Trying to convince Amber to leave with him would be an even harder task unless he could get her to love him as much as he loved her. Whatever he was going to do, he needed to do it fast! Before it is too late for them both…

BRITTANY

Brittany didn't know what had just happened. She has never in her life been that easy. Was he some kind of sex magician? How did she go from checking the club out to spread eagle on Red's desk? Reality hit her as she got the hell out of dodge. What was she thinking? Was she even thinking her body took over in her mind and just reacted to him? Like she had known him for years. What about Andrew? It did not matter since he was dead. Did this mean she was a devil? What was her game plan? How was she going to manage the situation?   Brittany needed a blunt to clear her mind and relax. She decided to take Storm on a car ride since it was such a good day. Brittany wanted to get her some good soul food, so she went downtown to EBO's restaurant and bar. That was her favorite spot to go when she was hungry and did not feel like cooking.

EBOs was everybody's favorite spot to eat and have a drink. Even if you wanted to gamble, they had slot machines in the bar. It was a good time and a good vibe at EBO's. Everyone was mostly from Fairmont or somewhere in West Virginia, so everybody knew everybody. There would be the occasional fight or altercation but nothing too serious. Everybody had a good relationship with each other. Ebo ran a good place, and it was like a haven for her customers. When Brittany came in, she saw a few regulars sitting at the bar, Brittany needed a shot of Patron bad because her hands were shaking, her heart was racing for some reason, and her pussy was wet. Oh Lord, she was having a stroke or a heart attack! Fuck shots, she needs the whole damn bottle! What did she get herself into? More importantly, what was she going to do about it?...

RED DEVIL

Dara was on stage doing the best she could. She was still getting familiar with everything; she was determined to make just as much money as the rest of the devils. She knew she would have to practice more. She did very well for herself being the newcomer and all. She was proud of herself.

"I told you confidence is much sexier than anybody part," Lisa told Dara.

"It wasn't as hard as I thought it would be." Dara was counting her tips.

"Wear your confidence every day. It's sexy." Lisa gave Dara a high five. Dara only had on a sexy black gown. She looked amazing.

"Girl, you dress like you are going to see your worst enemy!"

"Nothing makes a woman more beautiful than the belief that she is." A wise man told me that once.

"I need a shot of Hennessy and some food in my stomach. I am starving, does stripping always give you an appetite?"

"Yes, it does and so does this blunt." Lisa pulled a blunt out of her bra.

"No thank you, weed is not for me, plus it's a rule."

"When you obey all the rules you miss out on all the fun." Lisa laughed.

RED'S DEVIL'S

"What happened to the other new girl Brittany?" Dara was curious to know all the details. "I don't think she worked out. But don't worry, now that you are here; you are going to love it here. As long as you remember to be a woman with a mind, a bitch with an attitude, and a lady with the class you would be just fine."

"I couldn't wish for a better life than I already have now. Not to be nosey but it seems like there's more to you and Red, but you know about the women. It doesn't bother you?" Dara asked Lisa, wondering how she could share him so easily.

"How can I put it? Rarely does my light dim. He puts me in the light even when I don't want to be. It was like I was drowning, and he saved me from the fresh air. He knows my innermost desires and all my deepest fears."

"Well, there are plenty of beautiful women in the world, but you are more than that. You're elegant, gracious, and intelligent, I am just saying. You don't want to change anything in your life?" Lisa smiled again. "Don't be a woman that needs a man, be a woman that a man needs." Then Lisa walked off singing. Dara thought to herself every queen deserves a king but do not get it twisted, she could run her castle herself.

RED'S OFFICE

"So how was your first night? How do you feel about being a devil? Were the men respectable?" Red was looking at Dara as if she was his last meal.

"Yes, I liked it. I feel OK so far and yes, they were respectable. I was a little curious, I just spoke with Lisa and even though it is not my business, I asked her how she handled you with other women. You do not feel like you are holding her back from being happy?" "I licked it, so it's mine."

"What the hell does that mean?"

"Calm down Daring Dara. It was a tasteless joke. My apologies."

"Ok I was about to say, does that rule apply to all the girls?"

RED'S DEVIL'S

He laughed. "Not all the girls, just some, besides me and Lisa have an arrangement. Now I am done talking about that."

"I am falling in love with someone I have no business falling in love with. She is feeling them, and she possesses an incredible inner strength."

Dara didn't know what to think, was he referring to her or one of his other devils?

"Everything has become better since you walked into my life, Daring Dara. I can tell you are very kindhearted and caring. First time I heard you laugh I knew I wanted that in my life."

"I bet you say that to all the ladies Mr. Red."

"Just call me Red, Daring Dara."

"Ok Red, thank you for this opportunity. I cannot pay you for my car just yet."

"You do not owe me anything considering it paid in full. You are a devil now. You are my family and I take care of the people I love."

"I cannot repress my feelings. I must tell you how I feel about you for some reason. I notice a little mischief in your eyes. I could not take my eyes off you from the day that I saw you. God was showing off when he made you. I fell in love with the expressions in your eyes. The heart of a woman is the best mirror you can find."

"I am not as sexy as Lisa."

"Sexy is a state of mind and it can be in all shapes and sizes. It is different for every person. I could see myself falling in love with you for a million tiny things you do with you not even knowing you do them."

"Wow, you just said a lot. I think I am going to call it a night and have Fred walk me out. I will see you tomorrow, Red."

"I never want you to leave my side, but you look so good doing it. Have a good night, Daring Dara."

Dara had Fred walk her out to her fully equipped brand-new car. She was thinking about the things Red was saying to her or was he just thinking out loud? Who was he referring to when he said he was falling in love with someone, and he should not be? He could not have been talking about Lisa. Could he fall in love with her from their one night together? If he was falling in love with her, what about Lisa? Dara was not trying to step on anyone's toes or make any enemies. Dara did not need any more drama in her life, Trevor was enough. Now he no longer stressed her out, at least for the time being. Trevor was way in the back of Dara's mind right now. Her focus was on Red and his intentions. Was Dara ready to take Lisa's place? Could he be in love with her so fast? Stranger things have happened. Life is her sleeping with Red in his toy box. Being intimate with her, knowing there were other women. Is she cut out for the crazy life of a devil...?

Chapter 14

AMBER

RED'S DEVIL'S

Amber made her first move to get more information out of Yields. She called him up and said she was ready for her dinner date. She did her hair and makeup and got dressed to impress. Ready to play the cat and mouse game with Red's lapdog. Her mission was to get as close as possible to Yields. He would not be hard to seduce. He already thought he was in love with her. Amber knew she would never feel the same way about him as he felt for her. She would just use it to her advantage long enough to figure out what Red was up to and how to get away from it. "I am sure you know where I live, so giving you directions is pointless. I am ready whenever you are." Amber was looking at her window to see if he was already outside somewhere lurking.

" I am only a few minutes away; I will be there soon."

Amber checked her gun to be sure it was loaded. She still felt nervous about this. Amber could not fully trust Yields. He was Red's best friend. Better safe than sorry. Just in case he tried anything she would be prepared to defend herself. Yields pulled up in a red Hummer. He was nicely dressed and smelled good as hell. He was looking good for a white boy. Amber thought anyway she had no interest in white men. She stuck to what she knew best in her life and that was her hustle. A lot of her clients were white, but she was not part of their package; they all had their wildest fantasies. She made their fantasies come true and kept their dirty little secrets. She has secret recordings of all her sessions that no one knew about but her. It was her Plan B just in case anything ever went wrong. She would have leverage.

Yields opened the truck door for her and then climbed in on the driver's side. He headed to Muriel's, an Italian restaurant. Once inside, he pulled her chair out for her and poured her wine. He was such a gentleman. Amber was not sure if it all was an act or was he genuinely a good guy caught up with the wrong friend. She was about to find the answer to all her questions.

"Thank you for joining me and allowing me to get to know you better. It's like I saw my entire future flash before my eyes when I saw you. As silly as that may sound, being with you is exactly where I want to be."

RED'S DEVIL'S

Yields had this serious look on his face while pouring his feelings out for Amber. She was a little taken aback by Yield's confessions of love for her. It was more of an infatuation to ensure love.

"You don't even know me; how can you have all these feelings for me?" Amber wanted to hear what he had to say.

"Let's just say I wished for a better life than when I met you." Yields sip some of his wine.

"It was fate that brought us together, it wasn't your stalker psychopath boyfriend. I know you are taking a chance with me. I know I do not deserve it, but I will make it my priority every day to earn it."

"Wow, you got some smooth pick-up lines their Yields!" Amber thought this guy had to be joking.

"These are not lines; they are my true feelings for you. I know it is hard to believe, especially with me following you and investigating you, but you are what I never knew I always wanted."

"How do you think Red will feel about all these so-called true feelings you have for me?"

RED'S DEVIL'S

"Don't worry everything is under control, I can handle Red." Yields poured another glass of wine.

"Are you sure about that? Because to me, it looks like Red has just as much control over you as he does over his devils. I did my digging on your crazy friend. He is not such a nice person. He could even be described as an extremely dangerous man. So, what is his story? How did you two meet and become this dynamic duo?" Yields took a deep breath and said "We met in foster care, he lost his parents, and so did I. We are more than best friends, more like brothers. We looked out for each other. We had each other's backs since day one and 20 years later here we are. I will not say he's dangerous, just a little rough around the edges. He's a man of great power and even better resources. I know how to manage it."

"I guess we will see. Is there something you're not telling me?"

He sat up in his chair. "I am being completely honest about Red and everything else." The waiter came with their menus, and they ordered their food.

RED'S DEVIL'S

"So how will you get Red off my back for good?" Amber drank her glass of wine straight down then poured another glass.

"That is what I was going to talk to you about. I know you think I was tripping but everything I said to you is true. What if we just left Wesley and went somewhere to start a new life? I know you do not know me that well, but I promise when you get to know me, I'm a good guy. You are perfect. That's why I love you and you think you're not perfect makes me love you even more." Yields was quite serious.

"Wait a minute. You want me to leave my home and follow you halfway around the world to try to get to know you better and hopefully fall in love with you during all of this!?" Amber thought he was serious about all of it. This man was close to being obsessed with her period. Did she have to worry about him AND Red? "Don't you think that is a little far-fetched? I mean that's your plan to whisk me away to some foreign land and start a life with you? Are you serious right now?" Amber laughed."

RED'S DEVIL'S

"You are just as crazy as your friend!"

Yields did not think that was funny at all. "I am profoundly serious. Amber leaving this place with you is not all about Red. I want to build a life with you and have a future with you. Not one day passes that I don't feel my love growing for you."

"Listen Yields, I do not plan to run from Red. I'm not going to change my whole world for one man. He will not control me in any shape, form, or fashion. This is my home and I'm not going anywhere with you or him."

"You should just erase the idea from your mind. You have come up with another, better plan maybe we can talk. If you can't handle your friend, I will do it my way and on my terms." "I think you should take me home now. I have an early appointment in the morning." They left the restaurant and headed back to Amber's house.

"You sure you won't run away with me even if Red was not in the picture?"

RED'S DEVIL'S

"Yields, I am not ready to leave my business behind. It took me years to get to my status. I cannot just walk away from that, away from my friends, and family."

Yields knew she was right; it still didn't hurt to try. If only he could convince her their troubles would be over. Yields was not going to give up so easily. This was his soulmate, her home. If he was with her. Only if Red were out of the picture permanently then he could have Amber and build a future here in West Virginia. If only Red was not around anymore he could be free to love Amber without having to hide his feelings. Deep down Yields knew Red would not allow that as long as he lived.

Red wanted Amber and he was determined to get her. Nothing and no one would stand in his way. At first, it was a lustful infatuation that had hampered his attention. Now it's to prove to himself that he could have whatever he wanted. He let one girl slip away. Naomi was the only one to leave Red Devils. This is going to be the hardest decision Yields had to make in over 20 years of friendship. Yields and Red never fought over a woman before. Red always gave the

RED'S DEVIL'S

girls to Yields after he was done with them back in the day. When they were younger, it was like Yields was living in a Red shadow. Now it is time for him to be his own man and win the heart of Amber.

Amber had to produce a game plan. It was not going to be easy dealing with Red. She learned a lot from Yields tonight, at dinner. She planned to see him again very soon. Amber had one of her clients do some more digging on Red and her client would do anything for Lola who is Amber's alter ego. Amber was known in her business as Lola and Lola was every man's dream come true. When she got the car from her client, he sent her a flash drive with all she needed to know on there. When the flash drive was delivered, Amber couldn't wait to see what Red and Lisa were all about, and how could she use what she found to get rid of him for good. Without using any drastic measures, things started looking up for Amber. She knew she just had to play the game with Yields and in Red so let the games begin, Amber refused to be pushed around by Red or anybody else for that matter. She had to keep one eye on Yields.

How he may become another problem that she had to deal with. Eliminate all threats...

Chapter 16

RED'S DEVIL'S

BIG PAPA

Big Papa was checking the kitchen and prepping his food for tonight's menu. No one was ever allowed in his kitchen for any reason, not even Red. Big Papa had total control over the entire kitchen. Big Papa did his job very well and with pride. He was the best and he knew he was. For some reason, Big Papa thought he smelled perfume in his kitchen. Who broke his rule about no one in the kitchen? It was not just any perfume; it was white diamonds that Naomi used to wear. Was his mind playing tricks on him? He was just missing her too much or thinking about her more than usual.

He thought back to the first day Naomi came to Red Devil. She was the most beautiful thing Big Papa had ever laid his eyes on. Her body was out of control. She was all the woman he ever wanted and needed. Naomi and Big Papa grew remarkably close and then started seeing more of each other outside the club without Red's approval. One minute she was there and the next minute she was gone. Red never spoke a word to Big Papa about him and Naomi. Big

RED'S DEVIL'S

Papa never confronted Red about Naomi's whereabouts. No one said her name anymore after she left.

Big Papa would just pray that wherever she was that she was safe and happy. His love for Naomi could never fade or lose its power. Being with Naomi was like a cure for all the elements in his soul. Being surrounded by beauty and good pussy helped a little bit. He was still a man he could give another woman his body, but only one woman had his heart. That woman was Naomi. Big Papa had his choice of women and Red Devils. He would get private dances or jacuzzi rooms with a bottle of champagne. He had needs just like any other man. All his needs were met at Red Devils except one.

RED

Red was going on the monthly trip that he did so many times before. He has been taking these trips every month for 15 years. No one ever knew where he went or who he was with. Lisa did not even have that information. That's the only thing he ever kept from her in the 15 years. She used to try to get it out of him, but he would never tell her. He would just say taking care of some personal time to relax. It was his time for a vacation and peace of mind.

He left instructions as usual; he knew Lisa would run a tight ship while he was away. He knew he didn't have anything to worry about when he left her in charge. He knew Fred wouldn't let anything happen to his devils, especially Lisa. Fred had a love for Lisa as if she was his flesh and blood. Red called Yields to give him instructions to follow in his absence. He wanted results, he wanted Amber.

He had a love for Lisa and a desire for Dara and a hard-on for Brittany and an obsession with Amber. Any other man would get tired of trying to juggle so many women at one time. But not Red, there was enough of him for all the women in his life. He had plans for Amber. Plans he would not share with anyone. Not even his best friend Yields. Speaking of Yields, Red could tell that something was off with him lately. He was going to find out just what that was as soon as he got back from his trip. There was work to be done.

If Amber did not join him on her own, he would make it where she did not have any other choice. She was going to be a devil one way or the other, whether she liked it or not. She would have to learn to like it. She did not have a choice. Red was going to make Amber his and only his. He had a fire burning deep down in him for Amber, one that no woman in the past or future will diffuse. He had to have Amber in the worst way...

LISA (RED DEVIL)

At last, Red was out of the way; now Lisa could get work done. She needed information and since Red wasn't willing to share anything with her, she was going to have to get it herself. She was on a mission. Things were about to change. Red was beginning to rub Lisa the wrong way. He was getting beside himself with these new devils and the audition in the toy box. He had not taken anyone in the toy box in years, what was he trying to replace her with? Was she not useful anymore? Were they not a team? Whatever Red was doing Lisa did not like it at all. She would be damned if some new bitches off the street knocked her off her throne. She invested 15 years of her life with Red. No one was pushing her out. Lisa was not about to lose her investment; she had too much to lose and a lot more to gain. When she was ready to go, then she would leave with no problem. Until that time, she was still the headmistress of the Red Devil.

Her clientele was good and strong, and she dealt with a lot of men that had lots of money. She attracted a very wealthy crowd. Guys would pay for her to hope that they may have a real chance with her. She has even had three different men propose to her over the years. Some of the guys buy her expensive gifts and jewelry. They would pay for trips, bills, and shopping sprees. Lisa hadn't made it; she was still missing that one thing, her daughter. None of the devils knew Lisa had a baby. She got pregnant at the age of 15 and Red talked her into giving the baby up for adoption. So, Lisa laid eyes on her daughter only long enough to hand her to the nurse and the home. Lisa was still a baby herself. Red assured her it was for the best. The Red Devil was no place for a child or a worrying mother. He told her it was best for both of them. Lisa did not even get a chance to name her baby girl. All she remembered was a birthmark on the right shoulder of her daughter. It looked like a butterfly. When she looked at it. That was all she could remember.

For years Lisa believed that she had made the right decision, but now it seemed to her like the biggest mistake she ever made. Asking for help was out of the question. This was something she had to do on her own. The way he talked to her he cannot talk her out of it. Her daughter would be 15 years old now. Lisa tried to imagine what her daughter would look like today. She could be in the same room as Lisa, and she would never even know it.

Lisa had keys and combinations to all the rooms and was safe in the building. Now that Red was away, she could do some investigating. She sat behind her desk thinking if she wanted to hide something where

RED'S DEVIL'S

would she hide it? While she was sitting there contemplating, she noticed they posted notes on the floor under the Red desk. Lisa saw a piece of paper on the floor. Right as she was about to read it, there was a knock on the door. He hurried up and put the paper in her bra as Brittany walked into Red's office.
"Where's Red?" Britney sounded like she had an attitude, but she did not, that's just how she came off.
"He is not here. What is it that you need Brittany?"
"Hello to you too," Lisa said with half a grin on her face. "Hello, where is Red?"
"Out of town, did you come to finish filling out your forms, I'm sure Red would love that news when he returns."
"I am not here to fill out forms or to be a devil. I will be back." Brittany walked out of the Devil's office and closed the door. Lisa pulled the paper out of her bra and read it. Lisa could not believe Red was in Paris!

Chapter 17

FRED

Fred knows everything, sees everything and hears everything. He is the only security Red ever needed. Having a military background and training he was exceptionally good at his job and Red knew it and appreciated it. Fred knew most of Red's darkest secrets; no one was closer to Red than Lisa and Fred. He had to know those secrets to be able to protect Red. Fred even knew some things that Lisa thought she knew but didn't. Those secrets were kept because that way it was good for her safety.

Fred has been by the Red's side for 15 years since the first day he walked in the Red Devil with Lisa. She was so young and innocent, still a child, in Fred's eyes. He wasn't there to give his opinion, only to protect his family. Even though behind closed doors Fred would read his opinion. Red always respected Fred for what he did; he couldn't have found a better man for the job.

RED'S DEVIL'S

Fred watched Lisa grow from a little girl into a full-grown woman. He knew everything about her. He helped Red take care of her until she didn't need them anymore. Fred wouldn't hear of it; he would never stop protecting her. He would die for Lisa. Fred loved her too much to let someone hurt her.

He knew Lisa was ready to leave the Red Devil. She had not been herself in weeks. He could tell something big was on her mind. He could always tell when something was up with Lisa, or if she was planning to do something Red would not agree with. Fred just hoped that whatever it was that she would be very careful. Fred did not want to have to choose between Red and Lisa. Their situation never sat right with Fred; on this subject, he kept his opinions to himself. He bought it up one time 15 years ago and Red said it was never to be discussed again, so it hasn't. Fred knew which lines not to cross. He enjoyed his job and he just enjoyed being alive even more. Even though he had a bond with Red he knew Red would not hesitate to have him taken care of if he felt the need.

RED'S DEVIL'S

Fred chose to stay. He also had rules to follow. Fred knew the girls depended on him, and he would never let them down. Fred silently prayed that Lisa would get through whatever it was she was going through. And if it was what he thought it was, he prayed she would make it out alive...

DETECTIVE YIELDS

Detective Yields could not stop thinking about Amber. How beautiful she was, how good she smelled. He even loved the sound of her voice. He could not wait to see her again, so he invited her on a picnic out to Valley Falls. Amber agreed to go, she needed more information. She said she would meet him there so she can drive herself home when she is ready to go. When Amber showed up, Yields thought she was even prettier than the last time he saw her. When you realize, you are starting to fall in love with someone, you want your life to start as soon as possible. Yields was ready to start his new life with Amber. Yields thought love was passion and obsession; loving someone without whom you cannot live. Yields felt as if he could not live without amber in his life.

"Thank you for joining me, Amber. You look lovely as ever, I spend most nights at home falling in love with you and the idea of you." Amber blushed; she did not know why but she was blushing as she could not stop.

He thought her laugh was beautiful and her smile was beautiful. Everything about her was beautiful. She made the world a beautiful place and he was glad to be in it.

LISA

Lisa was sitting at the bar picking over her food and letting her drink water down. She was humming to herself. Fred walked over to her and put his hand on her shoulder.

"Hey baby girl, how are you feeling today?"

"I'm OK, Freddy bear. Just have a lot on my mind. That bass in the rear has pushed me to the limit. Things are going to change around here. I hate him! I swear to God!" Lisa threw her glass against the wall.

RED'S DEVIL'S

"Hey baby girl, do not let no man pull you down low enough to hate him. You're stronger than that and tougher than that or did you forget!? I couldn't love you more than I love you right now baby girl. You are made of magic only I can see. I am so proud of you. You have grown up. I did not understand what happened until I met you. I was just existing then when you came along, I was living and loving. All because of you baby girl, all because of you. Anything you need to talk about I am always here, and my lips are always sealed." He kissed her forehead and walked off.

Lisa knew she could tell Freddie Bear anything, but this thing was too big for even her to grasp. 15 years he has been going to Paris for one week a month, the place she dreamed of going to. The place Red promised to take her for 15 damn years! How could he do that? Why would he do that? What was she going to do about it? Why would he keep that from her? What was so secretive about him going to Paris? Why hadn't he taken her, he promised? All these unanswered questions. Her head felt like it would explode. She looked down and noticed her hands were shaking. She felt like she was about to start hyperventilating. She needed to catch her breath and get situations together. Lisa needed to unwind and try to relax, nothing like busting a goodnight nut to relieve stress. Lisa went into the toy box, took off her clothes, and turned on her porno on the big screen. She picked out a vibrator and enjoyed her own company.

BRITTANY

Where was Red? Why does she care? Why was she so damn angry? Was it because he was not there or because she gave a fuck and why should she? What was so special about Red? Did Lisa piss her off with that smart grin? She did not have a problem with Lisa, not yet anyway. Her problem is the way Red had her feelings.

Brittany could not believe it. She did not know what came over her. She knew she wanted it to happen again. That was the part that made her mad.

RED'S DEVIL'S

How she couldn't get him out of her head. This should not be happening. How did she let it happen? Maybe because she had just lost a childhood friend that was murdered over a drug deal gone bad right after losing Andrew so soon. That had to be it, she was stressed and Red helped her relieve herself. She just did not get enough relief.   Yes, she just needed to cum real soon or she would self-combust.

Brittany decided a couple of shots of Patron would have to do for now and a blunt. Anything to take her mind off Red. If that was possible at this point. Brittany started thinking about performing what Lisa asked her about. She never even read the forms; all she did was have orgasms on his big cherry oak desk. Fuck those forms, she was not signing any forms. She was not a devil. She did not know what she was at that moment. She felt like a crazy woman. Why did Andrew have to die? Why did he leave her alone? What was she doing? What kind of hole was she digging herself in?...

RED'S DEVIL'S

AMBER

Amber was very satisfied with her client for digging up all the dirt on Red. It would come in handy. Now she had some leverage on Red. She even found out a little bit about Yields as well. Now she could play their game period and she was ready to win. Either Red would leave her alone or she would deal with him. Right now, she had wishes to grant. It was time for Lola to get back to work and pay bills because they were not going to pay themselves. Then she would call Yields and make her move.

RED'S DEVIL'S

Chapter 18

DETECTIVE YIELDS

"I have an idea, we can act like you were in a terrible accident and you died, then he will stop looking for you."

"Are you crazy?! You watch too much TV." "First, you wanted me to leave my family and run away with you and hopefully fall madly in love with you, now you want me to fake my death? This is real life, not some lifetime movie!"

"I know it may sound a little far-fetched, but it could work. All you have to do is trust me. Everything will be all right." He told her, holding her hand thinking how soft her skin was.

"I trust you, but sorry I can't agree to that. I'm not going to be hiding for the rest of my life!"

"It won't be the rest of your life, just a short while." Amber was not sure what she should do. She would just go with it for now.

"Ok, give me some time to think about it." She scratched his hand.

Yields smiled; he thought his heart skipped a beat. He got her to trust him, now all he had to do was get her to fall in love with him and then get Red out of the picture...

FRED

Fred thought that he knew exactly what Lisa was planning. He knew this day would come. To tell the truth, he thought it would have happened sooner. Lisa was finally seeing who and what Red was. Fred knew this truth would hurt. He could only pray that Lisa was strong enough to manage what was to come. Most of all, would she be able to forgive him? It would crush Fred to have Lisa hate him. He has always been honest with Lisa besides that one secret. How could he tell Lisa? It would shatter her. Not telling her was just as bad as telling her. They both would have the same outcome. Fred asked himself if it was worth losing his baby girl. He prayed about this every day for 15 years. He was going to find out just how strong their bond was. Will he be able to handle losing Lisa for good? How can he make things right? Is that even possible with a secret like that?...

BIG PAPA

What was he going through? Every time he turned around, he thought he smelled Naomi. His mind was playing tricks on him. She had been on his mind a lot lately for some reason. Big Papa wanted to know what happened to her. If she was dead or alive. What happened between her and Red? Why did he allow her to leave? Why hasn't she contacted Big Papa? Should he stay the fuck out of it and just ask Red directly what happened? If anyone could tell Big Papa, it would be Red and of course Fred.

Big Papa knew Fred would know all of Red's secrets along with Detective Yields, Red's childhood best friend, his little errand boy. He knew one or all of them had the answers to all his questions. Hell, Lisa would know as well. Everyone knew about Red and Lisa. She always got her way with Red. Big Papa was sure that Lisa could know a secret or two. The only question was who should he approach? Or should he do some digging of his own? Do it down low until he has some kind of lead on Naomi's whereabouts. He could have detective Yields do it for a price. Would he be able to trust detective Yields? Big Papa knew Yields hands were not clean. Especially, having Red as a best friend. This just might be something he did on his own for now. He could hire someone that was not in the Red circle. If that was possible, was it time to find his Naomi? He could only pray he found good news...

LISA

Lisa went back to Red's office and locked the door behind her. She searched everything and everywhere. She knew all of his hiding spots and yet she found nothing. She did not even really know what she was looking for. Anything that was out of the ordinary or something she had not seen before. There was absolutely nothing but the slip of paper with Paris written on it with his flight information. Who could be in Paris, his parents? Lisa had to find out and she knew just one person that could help her. They could help each other.

"Hey Big Papa, how are you today?" Lisa smiled at Big Papa.

"Hey Lisa, you know me getting ready for this lunch hour, prepping my food." He was wiping off counters and appliances.

"You have family in Italy, right? You lived there before, didn't you?"

RED'S DEVIL'S

"My sister still lives there. I did stay when I was a child, but I have not been in years."

"Well, I need your help. I think we can help one another." Big Papa had no clue what Lisa meant.

"How can we help each other? What do you need me to do?"

"I am glad you asked. I need to find someone in Paris and if I am not mistaken you would like to know what happened to Naomi." Lisa had his full attention now.

"Hell yes, I have been dying to know what happened to her. "How can I help you? How would you find out?"

"Trust me I have my ways." Lisa smiles.

"Then I am down. Tell me what you need."

"First, I need this between me and you, not Freddie Bear, Red, or Yields. It's just between us, is that understood?"

Big Papa smiled and said, "Is that all?"

"No. I need you to find out who was on this flight and where did they go in Paris."

Big Papa was excited and suspicious at the same time. He wanted to finally know. But what or who was Lisa looking for in Paris? He would do anything to find his one true love. Even if it meant walking into the devil's playground. Why hadn't she offered up this help before? What was she getting out of it? Was this some kind of setup? He would have to move carefully while he helped Lisa and helped him...

Chapter 19

AMBER

RED'S DEVIL'S

Amber made a call to her client. He was the only black prosecuting attorney in Fairmont, West Virginia. He checked out a few things for her. Now she had even more leverage on Red and detective Yields. Amber knew exactly what she was going to do. It was time for her to fall in love with Yields or at least make him think she was falling in love with him. Then they can get what she needs, to get rid of Red for good...

TREVOR

Trevor was born in Charlotte, North Carolina. He moved to West Virginia in his early 20's. He liked to commute for family and friends.

Trevor met Dara at Walmart one day while he was doing some shopping. In the beginning, Dara did not know he was married; he was not wearing a ring. By the time he told Dara the truth it was too late, she was already under his spell. Trevor was very sexy light-skinned, grey eyes, and long wavy, dirty blonde hair. And was about 5'7"and weighed 180 pounds. He looked like an underwear model. Always looking good.

He was everything that she thought she wanted in the man except the already being married part. That is why she had to break it off with Trevor. She was not being fair to herself. Trevor was selfish and dark, and she couldn't take it anymore. Trevor did not agree with Dara's' decision. No one left Trevor. It was not over until he said so. Dara thought it was going to be that easy just to cut him off and walk away like he never mattered. Who did she think she was? He was nowhere near done with Dara. He was going to make her realize she had made the wrong decision, and he would hardly have to convince her. He would have to get her to change her mind to see things differently, then she would understand that they belonged together forever.

He knew eventually Dara would get tired of waiting on him to leave his wife. He just needed more time, but Dara could not understand that it just wasn't that easy. He loved Dara and he wanted to leave his wife and be with Dara, it just was not the right time.

RED'S DEVIL'S

Trevor's wife would try to take everything he had worked so hard for in the divorce. He refused to let her walk away with anything. He thought things would be better if she was dead. Then he can love Dara forever. He would prove his love today. She belonged to him and the sooner she realized that the happier they both would be.

Dara had not noticed that Trevor had been following her and watching her. He could not believe she was a devil. Trevor heard the stories; he'd never been there himself. He only knew what people told him. Trevor knew enough to know that Red treated his girls like private property. How did Dara get mixed up with Red and become a devil? He was going to put a stop to that. He hoped Dara had not betrayed their love by sleeping with anyone behind his back. Did she love someone else? Was she turning tricks for Red or with Red? How could she afford that brand-new car? She had to do something to drive an expensive car like that.

Trevor kept thinking about how good Dara smelled, how sweet she tasted, how giving she was when they made love, and how eager she used to be to please him. Then she started to change. Dara changed the rules. She started making demands and giving ultimatums. Trevor did not like whatever Dara was going through. It was some ridiculous behavior and she needed to stop the bullshit. He did not like this new Dara. He wanted his sweet, obedient lover back by his side where she belonged. She proved her point now it was time to come back. Game time was over.

Trevor was tired of waiting on Dara to come back to her senses, he would have to help her change her mind. He would have to show her what a big mistake she was making. Dara just wanted to get his attention and prove a point. Trevor thought she proved her point. He was finally going to leave his wife. He thought that would have to make Dara come back to him.

He didn't want to look for love and lose his hard-earned money in the divorce, but he couldn't live without Dara in his life. He had to get her alone and try to talk things out to convince her that they were meant to be together. Trevor watched Dara pull into the driveway and get out of her car, she unlocked the door and went inside then closed her blinds. Trevor couldn't see her anymore, so he pulled off and headed home. Thinking that he would have his Dara back soon...

Chapter 20

BIG PAPA

It is time to find his boo. First thing first, call his sister in Paris and get some information about someone in the Latin quarters. His sister used to be an assistant in the real estate business in Paris. She had quite the connections. She agreed to help Big Papa. His sister knew how head over heels Big Papa was for

RED'S DEVIL'S

Naomi. He called her all the time talking about Naomi, the girl of his dreams, the girl he was going to marry and spend the rest of his life with. She was there, and they were happy then she was gone, and it was like he shut down emotionally. Always had that nagging question in the back of his mind where was his Naomi? He had to know.

Just as he planned to search for by himself, Lisa presents a perfect opportunity to help him do just that. He had faith that Lisa was very capable of getting what she wanted from any man or woman for that matter. Lisa was the key to unlocking the Naomi mystery. It was like being excited about Nancy Drew books. Lisa gave him some credit card numbers to check. Lisa had a thing with numbers she could read any number one time she would never forget it. She knew every number on every credit card Red had. She knew that nerdy little gift would come in handy for her someday. Big Papa gave all the information to his sister, and she got to work.

His sister was eager to help him find the love of his life. Then he could be happy again. He had been walking around so sad and depressed. Like a damn zombie. Numb to everything around him. Now he had a reason to live and the motivation to go on. His sister needed to find an address in Chantilly Paris and property in the 7th district. Followed the paper trail and discovered the truth. This should be easy. She would have names, addresses, phone numbers, photos and so much more in no time. She was good at investigating. You would think of her as a new-age Carmen San Diego. She dated a detective for a few years, and he taught her a lot. He tried to talk her into going into the police academy. She liked the work, but she only did it as a weird little hobby. She did not want to do that full-time. Too much death and stress but when it came to getting information, she was your go-to person. Big Papa had confidence in his sister. The more she found out in Paris the better chance he would have of being reunited with Naomi.

Why did she wait so late to help? She did not need anything from him. He was her brother so of course she was going to help him; it was the right thing to do. Why would someone be so heartless? Everyone at

RED'S DEVIL'S

Red Devil knew how Big Papa felt about Naomi. If they didn't, they were blind, deaf, and dumb. Lisa knew exactly how he felt about Naomi and never did or said anything to help or answer his questions. Now she needed something from him so all of a sudden, she was eager to help him. No matter how messed up the situation was, there was nothing he could do to change it except to do his part and hope Lisa come through on her side of the bargain. He had been wanting and waiting for this for this long, a few more weeks could not hurt. Big Papa knew his sister wouldn't let him down.

He couldn't believe that he could be seeing Naomi again. He never thought he would have the chance to tell her how much he loved her and needed her. Meeting her was fate, but he had no control over falling in love with her. If he had only one hour left on this earth he would choose to be with Naomi. When Big Papa fell in love, he couldn't fall in love again. Falling in love with Naomi was the easiest thing he ever did. If he could have Naomi back in his life, he would leave the Red Devil and take her to

Paris and live happily ever after. He could get a job as a chef and make even more money than he is making at Red Devil. He could provide her with a good life. A new beginning. Never looking back and forgetting about Red, Red Devil, and all the secrets and lies that come with it...

DARA

Dara was exhausted and her feet were cramping from walking and dancing in six-inch heeled stilettos all night. A hot bubble bath with some Epsom salt sounded like a winner. She ran her bathwater, poured her a glass of wine, and lit a cigarette. That hot water was exactly what her body needed. It felt so good. She almost dozed off in the bathtub until she heard the doorbell ring. It startled her for a moment until she realized it was just the doorbell. She wrapped herself in the towel and went to see who could be at her door at 4:00 am. When Dora got to the door and looked out the peephole, she did not see anyone. She took the chain off the door and peeked outside. There were a dozen long stem red roses on her porch. They did not have a card. She thought Red was so sweet sending her flowers. He is surprising Dara. She wondered what exactly Red had planned for her. She put the roses in a vase and set them on the table.

Dara was still a little tender from her new devil horns tattoo. It did not hurt that bad. She looked in the mirror and she could not believe she was a devil, stripping and making enormous amounts of money. Time to find her a better place in a better neighborhood. She saw big things in her future. Being a devil was the best decision she had made since she left Trevor. Now she did not feel bad about herself anymore. She was not cheating herself out of happiness anymore. For a moment she thought of Red there giving her a full-body tongue-down. His head game was amazing. Good pussy eater does not eat pussy when they ask in the air; they lay down like a sniper. Red hit his target. Dara collected her tips of $3500 for her first night. Time to start saving so she could relocate to something bigger and better. She

RED'S DEVIL'S

drifted off to sleep thinking about the next time she went into the toy box.

Chapter 21

DETECTIVE YIELDS

"Did you think about my proposal? Not marriage, even though I would be honored Amber, but about faking your death and leaving." They were at EBO's eating catfish and fries.

"I need more time. I have been thinking about what you said. Well not just one thing but everything about how you feel about me. How you cannot stop thinking about me."

"I think I am beginning to have feelings for you too. I mean... I am not in love yet, but I have extraordinarily strong feelings for you."

"You are finally getting to me. Where I could see us together somewhere far away, starting a new life. The only thing in our way is Red. I want to feel safe, not worrying about if he is still out there somewhere hunting us down. I don't want to be looking over my shoulders for the rest of my life."

Yields held Amber's hand. "I promise you, my love, Red will not be a problem for long. I will manage him; I just need a little more time." Yields moved her hair out of her face and kissed her nose, and then her forehead then he kissed her hand.

"I love the way you make me feel. I am falling in love with you." Amber told Yields and squeezed his thigh then rubbed her hand up gently caressing his dick under the booth where no one could see. Yields was already rock-hard as soon as he sat next to her, he got hard.

"I'm falling in love with you more and more every time I see you." Yields was looking at Amber as if she were the only woman on the planet.

"When will Red be back from his trip?" Amber asked Yields as she sipped on her Sprite.

"He returns in two days." It's like clockwork every month. The last week of the month he is gone for exactly seven days."

RED'S DEVIL'S

"Once he gets back, I should have my plan ready and then I tell him our story about you being in an accident and I tell him I have a job offer to transfer out of the States and tell him I accepted the offer. I even have the paperwork from my office if he has any questions. I can have some obituaries printed up and bring him one as proof."

"That all sounds good, but will it work is the question?" Amber thought it all sounded ridiculous. But she went along with it.

"I will talk to him when he gets back and see how he is, and where his head is at least about the situation, and go from there. "

"If you are sure about it, then I'm in." He knows how Red gets when he had his mind set on something there was no talking him out of it. Yields had a job on his hands for sure. Changing his mind was no small feat. Yields hoped he was ready, he needed to be as convincing as possible. He hoped his best friend would go easy on this and find another girl to be his devil. If only Yields could find someone else for Red to set his sights on and forget about Amber altogether.

RED'S DEVIL'S

Yields had to protect Amber at all costs. He just found her, and he could not lose her. Red had enough women for two lifetimes. Why couldn't Yields just have one? He never asked for anything ever and Red never offered Yields any handouts. Yields was a hardworking man; he earned every dime. Nothing was ever just handed to him. They grew up on the wrong side of the tracks but still made something of their cells. They gave themselves a better life and a better future. Yields wanted his new future to include Amber...

RED

Red got off the plane and retrieved his luggage. He tore the baggage tickets off his suitcases and tossed them in the trash. He put his passport into a safety deposit box. Then he went to pick his car up out of the carport. Once he loaded his luggage in the trunk, he changed jackets and climbed into the front seat. Before he could close the door, someone came out from behind another car in all black with a black ski mask and black gloves started firing at Red. He was hit three times but managed to get in the car, close the door and smashed the gas. He still heard gunshots as he was getting the hell out of there.

After he drove a couple of blocks, he pulled over to check his wounds. He took off his jacket. Underneath his T-shirt there were 3, 9-millimeter bullets lodged into his bulletproof vest. That was one of the rare secrets no one knew except for Fred. His vest and his habit just saved his life. He did not see the gunmen's face, there was no way he would be able to identify him. He was wearing all black.

Who was gunning for Red? Was this an old enemy he forgot about or a new enemy he does not know about? He called Fred and explained the situation and let him know he was headed to Red Devil from the airport in Pittsburgh. He would have Fred get his car repaired. He could not drive around in the car with a full set of bullet holes. He knew he would not be calling the police and making a statement. He had his police to call. Yields was on speed dial, the only cop with which he would deal.

RED'S DEVIL'S

Yields would have to help Red figure out who tried to kill him and why. Red took that very seriously. Whoever was responsible was on borrowed time. If Red ever discovered their identity he would end them immediately. Red had too much to lose. He would not get caught slipping again for a while. He needed to keep an eye on all his surroundings and start paying closer attention to the people around him. Red just had the most relaxing seven days in Paris to only come back to this shit.

He could not wait to get back to the Red Devil. He needed to see Lisa; he missed her while he was away. He needed some play time in the toy box with his favorite playmate. Lisa or as he likes to call her Princess Diana, was a wild, sensual, lustful domineering woman. That was Lisa's treat for him when she felt he deserved a visit from naughty Princess Diana. Oh, how he loved her alter ego. Princess Diana did the nastiest, filthiest things to Red, had him begging for more.

He knew he had made the right choice when he picked Lisa. He groomed her over the years until she was ripe for the picking. She was his perfect creation. No other woman could compete with Lisa as his number one. She never worried about competition, that was until Dara and Brittany came into the pictur d Brittany was. Lisa didn't know how rare it was going to be to get Brittany. These two weren't any different from the other beautiful devils that worked for Red. Lisa did not know what was going on, but she didn't like his behavior lately. He had never been this way before. Lisa thought he was becoming more possessive and obsessed with the girls. Is he beginning to go a little mad? Slipping away from reality... what has come over him?

Lisa was not worried about being replaced; she would never let that happen. Did Dara or Brittany have a secret agenda? She would have to keep an eye on both of them to see what they were up to. Red's behavior was just a little too strange. Lisa would find the underlying cause of it.

Lisa was in the toy box cleaning and getting things ready for Red. She knew he would want to see Princess Diana tonight like he does every time he

RED'S DEVIL'S

comes from his monthly trips. She never really thought to search for clues about his trips to Paris in the toy box. As she was cleaning, she noticed the laptop on the shelf. Red only used it to make his private videos. Something told her to check the files. Nothing stood out, just homemade amateur porn. Then Lisa saw the file marked" Naomi". She was expecting to see a video of Rain and Naomi or Naomi and a special client.

Red had special clients that paid a nice price to use the toy box. He had secretly taped them while they indulged in their deepest darkest fantasies. Red was always two steps ahead of everyone else. He kept his tapes and files because he never knew when he might have to bribe someone or convince them to do whatever he needed to be done.

No one knew about the cameras except Red, Lisa, and Fred. There were cameras all over Red Devil. Lisa hurried up and sent a copy of Naomi's file to her email. Then cleared the history and pulled up the old porn they taped a while back. She showered and put on her long red boots. With her red shirt and red skirt, and corset with her crown. Princess Diana had long red fingernails, and luscious red lips, and those perfect titties had her nipple clips a vibrating tongue ring. Time to welcome Red back home, back to his castle Lisa went to the bed and climbed into the swing positioning herself upside down. Which happens to be her favorite position.

Red walked into the toy box and his dick instantly got hard. He was dropping his clothes on the floor like they were burning his skin. He could not wait to taste Lisa's soft, wet peach. He licked her from the pussy to her ass. He kissed her ass cheeks, licked them and smacked each one of them then he positioned himself to slide his dick in while she was spread eagle inviting him to come inside. Red took 2 E-pills. One he put on Lisa's tongue the other he pushed in her ass. He popped 2 pills himself then used his tongue to stick the E pill deeper in Lisa's ass.

Red entered Lisa. She was so wet and so tight he thought he would not last much longer. He flipped Lisa upright in the swing and took her from the back pulling the chain off her nipple clips gently but hard enough that her nipples were hard and throbbing for attention. He licked and sucked and teased her titties, then he did the same thing with her pussy. His pussy lips were so soft, and his mouth was so warm and wet, dick so thick and long.

Lisa climbed out of the swing and pushed Red back on the bed. She did the Chinese splits on Red dick and began to ride him up and down back and forth. Then she spent Red round and rode him backwards like a cowgirl. She was popping that ass and squeezing his dick with her pussy muscles. She sat on his face and squirted down his throat. While Lisa continued to ride his face, she leaned down and took him inside her mouth. She sucked his dick slow with wet lips and deep soft sucks Her wet hands were pulling, squeezing and twisting his dick, driving him so crazy he almost couldn't take it.

He was concentrating on sucking her pussy and eating her ass. He got up and went behind her. He grabbed her hips and hit her from the back, nice hard strokes then slow grinding strokes. He took his fingers and vibrated them in her ass while he hit the pussy; she squirted all over his stomach. Lisa then he put his dick in her ass and slid a dildo in her pussy; at the same time she was squeezing her titties and lightly pinching her nipples. He licked up and down her back and bit and sucked on her neck and shoulders. Lisa dug her nails into Red's satin sheets.

He kissed her neck and behind her ear and on her arms. Licking her thighs and sucking her pussy again. He handcuffed her to the bed and wrapped her long sexy legs around his neck. It felt like he was saying his alphabet in her pussy. She was having back-to-back orgasms and could no longer control her body. She needed to touch him, but her hands were cuffed. She begged him to be free, but he kept licking and sucking and teasing with his finger slowly in and out. Then licking her clit and licking her lips. Then slid his fingers into her mouth while she grasped his hand.

Finally, he took off the cuffs, so she pulled him on top of her and kissed him long and deep. She was rolling her hips while grinding against his pelvis trying to get all of his dick inside of her. Red cried out, pulled out and came all over her face and neck and breasts. Red collapsed on top of Lisa. That was one hell of a welcome home. Red got up and went to the shower. Lisa got some weed and the blunt out of the nightstand drawer and rolled up one.

She lay on the bed thinking about what was on that Naomi file. She would soon be finding out. It was about time to check with Big Papa and see if he had anything for her. As long as Big Papa kept his mouth shut about their arrangements everything should be ok. Red got dressed and went into his office, he had a phone call to make. Time to see what Yields had for him. He was hoping it was some good news. He wanted Amber and he was determined to have her. If she knew what was good for her, she would give in to Red. It would make things a lot easier for both of them. Red would be a happy man because he would have everything he wanted, a girl for every day of the week. We'll start with Moanday, Touchday, Wetday, Thirstday Freakday, Sexday, and Suckday. Why shouldn't we be able to have whatever we wanted? That is why he had lots of money so he could afford whatever he wanted and then some.

Chapter 22

LISA

Lisa went home and got right on her computer and opened her email. She opened the name file. Lisa could not believe it. There were a few shots of her and a big pop-up here, all of her background information and one thing that stood out, a picture of a remarkably familiar face that Lisa grew to know over the last few years. If memory served her correctly, the man was in Naomi's file was her brother Arab, he was Naomi's brother. It looked as if he had an agreement with Red about his sister Naomi. She was never to get involved with Red for any reason whatsoever. And looks like Red did not hold up his end of the bargain.

Is that why she disappeared? Did it have anything to do with the broken agreement? Where was she? Someone had to know. Lisa should reach out to Arab, then again that might not be such a good idea. Arab was an extremely dangerous man. Whatever he had over Red must have been noticeably big for Red to be in business with Arab.

All Lisa knew about Arab was he had a business situation with Red. Now she had to find out just what kind of connection they had. There was still no clue where Naomi was and if Arab ever knew his sister was once a devil even for a brief moment all hell would break loose.

Something had to happen for Red to send Naomi away. Or did she leave on her own? Why did Red go against Arab and hire Naomi anyway? She had to figure out what was going on. From the looks of it, it looks as if Naomi got herself pregnant then she just vanished without a trace. Now it is up to Lisa to find Naomi and find all the answers to her unanswered questions. Lisa wondered if Arab found out and was responsible for the attempt on Red's life tonight at the airport? ...

RED'S DEVIL'S

FRED

Fred took Red's car in to be repaired then pulled out Red's royal blue BMW to drive until his car was fixed. Red had a fleet of cars of different colors and models; he even had three customized Harley motorcycles. Red wanted Fred to boost up security a little more for the time being until he could figure out who tried to take him out. Someone knew what time his flight landed and where he was parked. Luckily, he was a creature of habit and always wore his vest when he was traveling. That was something Fred had him doing for years. This was not the first time his vest saved his life. You could say he owed Fred his life. He knew he picked Fred for a reason.

Lisa and Big Papa did not know Fred overheard their conversation in the kitchen. He had a bad feeling about what was going down in the Red Devil. Fred always knew everything that went on inside that club. A good thing he did not, he would have to figure out a way to protect Lisa from the shitstorm that was about to come. He had to come up with a plan fast...

RED'S DEVIL'S

DETECTIVE YIELDS

"Tell me that you have good news for me," Red asks Yields.

"Listen, I've been working on it, but my caseload has been overloaded. My captain Ben is on my ass. It is like I was putting more work in for you than at the precinct. I have kept a close eye on her but there is nothing really to tell she's just a regular chick working on her loft with her sexy high-profile client list."

"She works for herself and she's 28 and her parents are alive, she has two brothers and sisters, and she has a connection from Detroit that she deals with for her marijuana. She helps her mom with bills and groceries. She runs errands for her mom, and she is not involved with anyone at the moment."

"Ok, ok, well now I need you to approach her and give her my offer."

"And what am I supposed to do if she turns me down? Or turns you down and does not want to be a devil? We cannot force her or take her against her will. I mean really, what is your plan?"

Red stood up and walked around his desk. "Just approach her with my offer and tell her she can make three times what she is making now, and I will let her keep her clients as long as she agrees to be a devil. If she refuses, then I will handle it."

Red walked up to his safe, opened it and pulled out two stacks of money, and handed them to Yields. "Why don't you take the vacation days you saved up so you can focus on the task at hand? I need results and I need them fast. I have some new investors lined up and I want the sexiest, prettiest, most attractive women in the state right here at the Red Devil."

"I have a reputation for having only the best. And I am working on Brittany, but I need Amber here. She is going to be my new breadwinner with all the clientele she has. We could do great things together. I just have to make her realize that her place is here at the Red Devil. So, give her my offer, then find out who had balls enough to try to take me out and fucked the job up so horribly. I want them found and dealt with like yesterday!" He slammed his fist down on his desk.

"Ok Red, I will work on it. I will approach Amber tomorrow and let you know what she says." Yields walked out of Red's office and headed back to Ambers to tell her Red's offer. He knew there was no way in hell she would accept that offer or any offer from Red. Yield's future wasn't looking so bright for him from where he was sitting...

Chapter 23

BRITTANY

Brittany threw on some sweats and a wife beater, then put her hair in a ponytail and threw on a baseball cap and a pair of Jordans. She grabbed her keys, kissed Storm, and headed out the door on her way to see Red. Her body was on fire for Red. She needed him to touch her, fuck her, kiss her, and at some point, she needed to breathe his air. Was Red's dick that good? The pull was so powerful that Brittany started to think he put some sort of voodoo spell or curse on her. She has never behaved this way in her life or anyone ever!

RED'S DEVIL'S

None of that mattered now she knew what she wanted, and she knew just who she wanted it from. Brittany is concrete. She loves to cum. That is her favorite thing to do besides making money. With Red, she lost count of how many times she came back-to-back multiple times. She stopped counting after nine and she could no longer concentrate after that. She was cumming as she drove thinking about what he was going to do to make her cum some more. She was driving as fast as she could praying, she wouldn't get pulled over, kill herself or someone else while trying to rush to Red.

"What about this devil Shit?" She had forgotten all about the devil part, all she concentrated on was Red. Everything else was irrelevant to Brittany at that moment. Fuck those forms and his stupid ass rules. She does not have time for that. She needed to bust a few nuts then she would feel much better period.

Why was she acting this way? This is pure insanity! Long losing Andrew must have finally made her snap. Maybe she was just trying to fill that empty hole in her soul. Brittany could be using sex to deal with her sadness, to help keep her mind off of all the bad emotions she was trying to hide from. Red was helping her relieve some heavy stress.

Fred watched Brittany park, escorted her into the club, walked her to Red's office, and knocked on the door. Red told him to come in. As soon as he saw Britney his whole face lit up like a Christmas tree. One of his newest conquests.

"The thing you think of as your flaw is the reason, I am falling in love with you."

"Take your clothes off, I need you in my mouth now!" Britney began to undress frantically.

Brittany pushed Red against the wall, got down on her knees, and took him in her mouth deepthroating him. Taking him all in with each lick and suck he got harder and harder. Brittany was getting increasingly turned on herself. She was about to cum, as she felt Red's dick throbbing in her mouth and she was ready to explode. She stood up, turned around and grabbed her ankles. She was so wet her pussy was actually dripping. He smiled as he put his cock in and began pounding her phat ass pussy while squeezing her ass cheeks and pulling her hair. He pounded faster and faster until he felt her reach her point of no return then they came together. They were both weak in the knees for a moment.

That is exactly what she needed. What she had been waiting for. She could never get enough of him. She was insatiable when it came to Red. Brittany did not understand why but she liked the way he made her feel. If she had to become a devil just to be able to cum as much as she wanted, whenever she wanted, it just might be worth it. What was she thinking? She was not thinking, at least not with her head. More like between her legs is what was doing the thinking for her. She needed to focus and clear her mind of all freaky thoughts for a moment while they discussed her being a devil. He had not told her about the tattoo part yet. That part might not settle with Brittany. She would not want to be branded like the rest of the girls. She was nothing like them. She was her own person. She might not make as much as Red was offering but she was not struggling either. Why couldn't she just fuck Red when she felt like it and went on about her business? She did not have to be a devil to fuck his brains out.

Brittany was not good at following rules, which is why she made her own rules. That is why she never answered to anyone ever. Things were going simply fine until she bumped into Red. Now her whole world was turned upside down. She was doing things way outside the box. She thought she was losing control of herself in a good but scary, unfamiliar way. She needed to get it together fast. This was out of her character. What was she doing? She was getting crazy quickly....

AMBER

Amber had a decision to make. Playing along with Yields seemed to be going well. She just needed a little more time before she would make her move. The more time she spent with Yields the more he began to grow on her. She could not tell if she was catching feelings for him or not. She had only dealt with one white guy, and she swore to herself that she would never be with another one again. Only now, Yields was here in her life. He was becoming a permanent fixture.

Amber could not afford to get too close to Yields. The last thing she needed right now was a relationship. She was beginning to feel like she was in one with Yields. Always seeming to be there expressing his feelings, looking into her soul. Confessing his love for her was cute to Amber but she had no rules on relationships with guys that were white. If this went down Yields would be her first…

Chapter 24

ARAB

Arab was just as ruthless as Red, some said. Even more dangerous. He owned construction businesses, and he was an architect. Arab had designed many of the known buildings around West Virginia, his hometown as well as Cleveland, Ohio, the area of

RED'S DEVIL'S

Naomi's adopted brother. He was very overprotective of Naomi. Arab felt that no man was good enough for his baby sister. It was hands-off for everyone except him. He always had his way with Naomi.

Arab was sexy with light brown skin, brown eyes, 5 foot 11 inches, and 165 pounds. He had a sexy smile and a powerful presence. You knew when he entered the room. He always smelled good and looked even better in his three-piece suit and his fresh pair of Gators spending like 1,000,000 dollars and worth so much more.

He had a business arrangement with Red; He could have any woman except Arab's half-sister Naomi. She belongs solely to him. He raised her after her parents died and he became her legal guardian. Arab took care of her in every way possible. She was his special little doll baby to play with whenever he felt needed. Now she was missing, and no one had seen a trace of her. Arab had his people tirelessly searching for Naomi. He had to find out precisely what Red knew about Naomi's disappearance. He needed to bring his sister home safely where she belonged. He didn't care what it cost or what it took. He was determined to get back his favorite toy.

No one was allowed to play with Naomi except for him. If he had ever found out about Big Papa and Naomi, Big Papa would have to pay the price. If Arab discovered that Naomi ever visited the Red Devils, Red would have a hell of a fee to pay. Arab was not a man you wanted to cross. Some of his enemies were said to be buried under some of his most famous buildings. No one would ever know the truth behind that except for Arab. Many people have gone missing under suspicious circumstances, but Arab was never questioned about them. It was said that he had a powerful support system from the police and politicians to those working under him.

Time to put some of his power to use and find Naomi.

To find Naomi, Arab felt should start a little closer to Red's home and begin with Yields. He may be able to produce some answer, and perhaps he could help Arab locate Naomi. He knew Yields did anything to help Red and keep him out of jail. Why not do a favor for a good friend? A wealthy good friend. It would be in their best interest to cooperate to the best of their abilities If they knew what was good for them. Arab grew angrier as the days turned into weeks, months, and years. But he was not going to give up. As much as he loved Naomi, if she disappeared willingly, she would have to pay for her betrayal. He knew that if she made herself disappear, she had to have some help. He controlled her allowance, so he knew she had no money and to disappear she would need financial support. Someone had to help her. So, someone knew where she was, and someone would pay. When he found out who was involved in helping her disappear, they were in a shit load of trouble. Their days were numbered.

RED

"I got the car from Arab. He's looking for Naomi. I knew this day was coming. I need you to do a favor. I need you to check on something for me." Red told Yields he was distraught.

RED'S DEVIL'S

Red did not want any problems with Arab. He had enough on his plate to be bumping heads with Arab. Red did not need that kind of heat at the Red Devil. He was seen as a god by the Red Devil, and no one would change that

He had to make a phone call he prayed he would never have to make. Red had to call Big Papa's sister, Kathy, in Paris." Where is the girl?" Red was almost whispering.

"Why are you calling? We agreed no more contact except for your monthly checks. I should not be hearing from you. That was the deal!" Kathy was upset. They had an agreement, and Red just broke it.

"Trouble is coming. Papa is fine for now."

"For now? What's going on?"

Red took a deep breath. Arab is looking for his sister. You have to keep her safe. Find a new place, I will handle the cost. How is the girl?"

"She's fine. Do I need to worry? What about my brother? You told me I would not have to worry. It's your job to protect her." Kathys mind was racing. Red had her scared. Would she be in danger? Is her brother in trouble? She had to protect the girl at all costs.

" I'm handling things. I'll be in touch. Find a new place, do it now!"

Red hung the phone up. He never realized Lisa was in the toy box listening to everything. Pieces of the puzzle were beginning to fall into place. Red had to get this shit under control. He had time to cover his tracks. He didn't like how things were playing out. He had to get a wrap on this situation.

BIG PAPA

Big Papa got the information from his sister Kathy, now to pass it on to Lisa. Hopefully, she had some news for him as well. Big Papa knew his sister was busy with his niece, so she was doing him a big favor. Big Papa was desperate to find out what had happened to Naomi.

Big Papa told Lisa where the two properties were in Paris, and his sister was still digging. She told him about the conversation she overheard and Red's office. Maybe he was hiding Naomi in Paris. That's probably why he never took Lisa to Paris as he promised, so she would not find out about Naomi. Lisa's cogs were turning, who could he be seeing every month in Paris? He's been going to Paris for 15 years. It couldn't be Naomi; she had only been gone for about 5 years or a little longer. Did he move her to Paris? Is it one of the properties? Highly Naomi? Who's at the other property? Lisa still has so many unanswered questions. So did big Papa. Any news right now was good news to him. He would be one step closer to finding his love.

His super possessive brother Red had tried to warn Big Papa not to get mixed up with Naomi, but it was too late, they were in love. Papa would never forgive Red if he learned about Red's secret, even if what he did saved Big Papa's life. He was family, and Red protected his family.

Papa didn't know his sister had a secret just as significant as Reds. Kathy felt she had to save her brother and help the girl. If he found Naomi, he would never let her go again. Now he had to wait for his sister and Lisa to find more information. Big Papa was determined to find Naomi no matter what. He never needed to know the truth. He didn't know that Arab was also looking for Naomi, and his first stop was the Red Devil.

FRED

Fred and Lisa were digging around, trying to find out where Red had been going and who he'd been going to see for all these years. And now he was trying to find an army for Big Papa. But first, he had to find a way to convince Lisa to give up her search. It would only lead to a bad thing. Fred knew Red's secrets. This secret could not only devastate Lisa, but it could change everyone's lives forever. Fred just wanted to protect Lisa from being hurt. He cared about her a little too much. If Arab ever found out, everyone would pay for Red's sins and Fred couldn't let that happen.

Lisa was innocent. She had no clue about any of it, but she was getting too close to the truth that would best be left buried. How could he protect Lisa and still keep this horrible secret? There must be something he could do. Arab was not a man you crossed for any reason. He took everything seriously. Suppose he didn't like it. He had it removed permanently. Fred knew he had to help Red protect the secret for everyone's good. Fred knew precisely the kind of man Arab was. The kind that did not put up with any shit. Fred fought in two wars and n6ow it looked like he was about to fight another one.

Chapter 25

DARA

Dara was starting to get strange hang-up calls. It was weird enough that there were love letters and greeting cards left on her car and teddy bears inside of it. At first, she thought the gifts were Red's until the hang-ups started. Now she had no clue who it could be. Dara was beginning to get a little worried. She told Red and Fred about it. Red promised that he would take care of it and keep her safe. Dara couldn't believe she had a stalker.

LISA

Lisa knew where Red was going but not whom he was seeing. How could he lie like that to her? Lisa thought she and Red were on the same level but obviously she thought wrong! He was keeping secrets, and that was one of their rules. No secrets of any kind. Now she's finding out that he had more than one secret he was keeping from her. This only made her furious! She was going to find her answers.

TREVOR

Trevor knew Dara had to be fucking Red and who knows who else. He wasn't buying new cars off the lot, getting them fully loaded and customized just because he was a nice guy. Dara had to be fucking him, and Trevor wouldn't stand for it! Dara belonged to him! How dare she betray their trust and be with another man. If she thought she could leave him, she was mistaken. No one left Trevor...no one! Dara was going to realize she belonged with him. He was the only one who could love Dara the way she needed to be loved. Trevor knew no other man would treat Dara right. They would use her and neglect her. She came a long way from being insecure to being this dominant, lustful devil overnight. Red must be trying to brainwash Dara. Trevor wasn't going to have that.

ARAB

Arab was about to take a trip to West Virginia. He gave Naomi time to come home on her own. It had been five years since he saw his beautiful sister. He refused to sit by longer, not knowing his sister's fate. His first destination was the Red Devil. Time to talk with his dear friend, Red. If anyone could help him find his sister, it would be Red. He was good at that sort of thing. Finding lost stuff or people.

Arab couldn't imagine what was happening to Naomi or what she's been doing for these five years. First, he had to find his sister, his playmate. He needed to see, smell, and taste her beauty, he had been deprived long enough. He wanted to play with his Nubian Princess. There was so much he wanted to teach her and show her. Things he couldn't wait to do to her. It was time to teach her a lesson about misbehaving and disobeying him. She was going to learn her lesson. Arab was going to make sure she could never run off again.

KATHY

Kathy was a big girl, like her brother. She was 5 foot 6 inches and weighed 200 pounds. Dark chocolate eyes and a dark complexion. She had an arrangement with Red., Now Big Papa had her trying to find who owned these properties in Paris and where Naomi was. Kathy knew if one of these properties belonged to Naomi, it would expose the secret. Then she would have to tell the truth to her brother. If Arab ever found her, she would be in danger along with everyone else. It has something to do with her disappearance.

Kathy decided she had to tell Red before things got out of control. She might even risk it all until her brother speaks the truth. Kathy had a lot to figure out in a short amount of time. How could she keep her baby brother safe? The first thing was to find a new place. She had to keep the girl safe. Kathy was afraid. She didn't know how ruthless he was, only from what Red told her. If any of it was true, Kathy had a lot to be scared of.

She did more digging and found the names of the properties in Paris. They belonged to Beatrice Payton. Kathy had no clue who that was. Just that she was an elderly lady in her early 60s, she didn't work, but she kept a healthy bank account. She had a healthy sum being deposited every month. Kathy wasn't sure if she should pass this information on to her brother or try to bury it so no one would ever know. How could she get her brother to let it go? This is a can of worms

RED'S DEVIL'S

Kathy did not want to open. Finally, Kathy decided she would give the information to Big Papa. It was time he knew the truth, and now! Little did he know that he had hidden dangers around him.

ARAB

"So, you have not seen a Naomi or heard from her?" Arab asks Red, and he lit a cigarette even though Red didn't allow smoking in his building.

"No, I haven't, but I will have Yields investigate and try to locate her. Her Social Security number has no hits, no utilities in her name, no job, or social media. She is completely off the grid. I will let you know when I gather more information. You didn't have to make a trip. I could have called you."

"I like to do my business face to face. I like to look into a person's eyes when they talk to me. I can't see nervousness over the phone. I need to see the person. I'm speaking with. I know Yields has been with you for years. Do you think he's up for the job?"

RED'S DEVIL'S

"If she's out there, he will find her, but she doesn't want to be found then what?"

"That's neither here nor there. I want my sister back. I want what's mine!" He flicked his ashes on the floor.

"As soon. As I have something useful, I will be in touch." Red pulled an ashtray from his drawer and slid it too Arab.

"I will be here for an extended visit; I thought I would keep myself occupied at Red Devils. I want to unwind a bit and have a little fun. Your girls always find ways to keep me entertained. Besides, I heard you had some new merchandise. I've decided to stay and play for a while. I'm a little hungry. I like that chef of yours, Big Papa if I'm not mistaken, he is quite the chef. Have him whip me up something good while I pick my playmate for the time being. I expect Yields to put his full attention on finding Naomi. I want to wrap this up as soon as possible. I don't want to get my hands dirty unless necessary."

DARA

RED'S DEVIL'S

Dara didn't know if she was being paranoid or not. It felt like she was being watched. Red had a guy come by to follow her to work. She jumped in the shower to get ready for work. When she got out of the shower, there was a panty and bra set laid out on her bed. She knew she did not put it there. Someone had been in her house while she was in the shower. They went through her things. This was beyond scary. She hurried and got dressed, grabbed her back and rushed out the door. What was going on? Who is harassing her? What kind of game were they playing? She would have to talk to Red again. Fred escorted her into Red Devil and walked her to Red's office.

" Daring Dara, what can I do for you?" Red stood up to greet Dara.

"Someone was in my house earlier while I was showering. I don't feel safe. Do you think it could be one of my customers? I'm terrified; maybe this wasn't a good idea." Dara rubbed her left shoulder where the devil horns were tattooed.

"Trust me, beautiful; I will manage it. Pack your things and be ready to move. I have an empty property no one is using; you can stay there. If you don't like it, I will find you something more to your liking. Let me know what you need. Do you have anything for protection?"

Dara held up her key chain. There was some pepper spray dangling on her key ring.

"I was thinking of something more lethal. We will get you a permit and take you to the range so you can get some practice. I need you to be able to look out for yourself with me or Fred, who is not around. Are you sure? It's no crazy ex?"

Red looked at Dara. He could tell she was shaken up about the whole situation.

"No, my ex is married; he's not thinking about me. I don't know anyone else it could be. It has to be someone from the club."

Dara had never used a gun before. She never needed a weapon. She never felt as unsafe as she did now. Dara hoped she never had to have a reason to use a gun. Whoever was stalking her had her full attention. She just wanted this to be over. Picking up and moving was not in her plans, not at the moment.

She felt as if she didn't have a choice. Better to be safe than sorry or end up dead by the hands of some obsessed pervert. It could be any of the guy's Dara met during the weeks she worked at the Red Devils. How would she be able to figure out who it was? She was sure it wasn't Trevor. He would have no reason to stalk her. He chose his wife, so to Dara that meant he had no use for her anymore. Someone was following her, and she was scared to death.

Chapter 26

LISA

As soon as Lisa read the name on the property, she knew precisely to whom it belonged. Beatrice Peyton was Red's mom. She was the closest thing he had to a family, but she was dead. Or at least that's what Red told Lisa: his parents died when he was young. That's how he ended up in foster care. So how would she have a property in Paris? And why was Red lying about Paris? Who was he visiting all this time? Was he hiding Naomi in Paris? What was the big secret about Red? His mother, Paris, and Naomi? How could any of this help her find her daughter?

BIG PAPA

"How have you been, Arab? Got your food right here just how you like it. Hope you enjoy it."

"I'm sure I will; you have never disappointed me, and I hope you never will. I need to know if you know anything about my sister. Her name is Naomi. Here is a picture of her. Have you ever seen her in here?" He slid the picture across the table to Big Papa.

"I don't believe I've ever seen her come in here." Big Papas handed the image back to Arab. Are you sure about that, Big Papa? You never cooked for her? She has never worked here before?" Arab was staring at Big Papa.

RED'S DEVIL'S

"No, I'm sure I would remember."

"I'm sure you would. She is a very unforgettable person. If you suddenly remember something useful, I will let you hold on to this picture. I'm apprehensive about my sister. I'm sure you can understand that, coming from such a big family. I need to bring her home safely. I'm willing to pay for any information you may or may not have. I suggest you contact me immediately if you do find out anything. I want to keep this between the two of us for the moment. I'm going to enjoy my meal. I hope to hear from you soon. Enjoy your night, Big Papa." Arab took his plate and walked out of the main to the main floor to enjoy a good meal and a good show. Red called Big Poppa to his office. Could you have a seat? Do we need to talk?

"I'm sure you know Arab is here looking for Naomi. He can never know that she was here or anything about your relationship with Naomi. It's for everyone's good."

"I didn't say anything; I remember what you told me. Do you have any information on Naomi?"

RED'S DEVIL'S

"No, nothing, we just have to convince Arab we don't have any useful information so he can return to Cleveland. The sooner he leaves, the better for everyone. Stick to our story, and everything should be OK. Fred said Lisa asked questions about Naomi. Don't tell her anything. She doesn't need to be caught up in this mess. I don't need her digging around while Arab is here."

"OK, I got you. I won't say anything. But I will keep my eyes and ears open." They shook hands, and Big Papa left Red's office. He thought that the shit was about to hit the fan.

YIELDS

"I may have some information for you. This Stays between us and has no mention to anybody that you and I ever had this conversation. Red knows where Naomi is. She worked here for him briefly, and Red helped her disappear. I don't want any harm coming to me or my lady friend, her name is Amber; she has

RED'S DEVIL'S

nothing to do with Red and knows nothing about Naomi. I will help you find your sister; you will help me and Amber disappear. I want to be as far away from Red as humanly possible. We are looking for a fresh start, and that takes money, something I know you have plenty of. We can help one another, and Red wouldn't have the slightest idea."

Arab thought about this rare opportunity for a moment. This could be the lead he needed that is if he would trust that Red's right-hand man would betray their 20-year friendship to run off with some woman. Arad didn't care what the reason was; all that mattered was Yields was desperate and in love—two powerful weaknesses. Yields just might be precisely what Arab needed, but a desperate man is willing to do anything for love, even if it means selling out to your best friend.

   Yields was tired of being an errand boy for Red, cleaning up all his messes. Stalking potential devils and all the other bullshit he did for Red. He wanted a life with Amber. Free of Red. He was tired of keeping Red's hands clean and getting his dirty. Enough was enough. Time to live his own life with his soul mate. Time to take out the trash once and for all. Yields knew there was no turning back; now, he had to finish what he had started. If he wanted to be happy with Amber, he must eliminate Red. It was the only way they could be together and not have to look over their shoulders for the rest of their lives. Unfortunately, the only way that would happen was over Red's dead body.

FRED

"I need you to stop digging. It's not safe for you anymore. You know, Red is a man of many secrets. Just let this go, baby girl. It's for your good. Let me protect you." Fred held Lisa's hand.

"I can't do that, Freddie bear. I have to know. Red and I don't have secrets. Not like this. Why is it so wrong to find Naomi? What's the big deal?" Lisa pulled her hand away.

"Arab is a huge deal. Naomi was never supposed to be here, let alone work and be in a relationship with anyone. Arab has strict rules when it comes to Naomi. If those rules are broken, there will be hell to pay. I don't want you caught up in any of Red's bullshit! It's not safe. You have to think about Big Papa as well. He's family; we have to look out for one another. I know you're trying to discover what Red's monthly trips are about, but you must stop looking and let this obsession go. Listen to me, baby girl. I'm trying to help you!"

Lisa turned her back to Fred." You know, all Reds secrets? You know that he goes to Paris once a month. You have always known and realized he had properties in his mother's name. I'm almost positive you also know who he goes to see in Paris. If you know all that, you must know where Naomi is and what happened to her. Is there anything else you're not telling me?"

He was covering up all Red's skeletons. It's time to clean the closet. Why would Red endanger us and drag us into this shit with Arab? Why cross the man like that, knowing what was at risk? How could he be so stupid? Lisa said she couldn't understand why Red would do such a thing.

Red did not know Naomi was Arab's sister until after her audition and her devil horns branded on the back of her shoulder. By then, she and Big Papa were in love. Red had to move quickly to get her out of there and leave no trace. He knew what kind of man Arab was and about the things Arab did to Naomi. Couldn't you read it? Red felt sorry for her and helped her disappear. She had already endangered Big Papa by starting a relationship with him and dancing at Red Devil. Red betrayed Arab to save Naomi and Big Papa. Red took care of everything to help her escape from her brother."

"I know there is something you are not telling me. You know everything that goes on in Red Devils. Please help me by telling me the truth. Can't you see I'm hurting? I can't let this go. I have to know, damn it!"

Lisa stormed off, leaving Fred standing there, wishing there were an easy way out. How could he stop the truth from coming out? How could he protect

RED'S DEVIL'S

Red and Lisa? What measures would he have to take to ensure Lisa's safety? After all, he was her Freddie Bear, and she was his baby girl. He didn't want to keep the truth from Lisa. Some secrets were best never to be told. Especially this secret. It wouldn't do anybody any good. If Lisa ever found out just how much Fred knew. He didn't think things would ever be the same between them. That's a heartbreak for which he was not prepared.

KATHY

Kathy had to call Big Papa and tell him what she knew. She feared something terrible would happen to her brother if she didn't. She couldn't trust Red anymore. What if he gave up big Papa to save his ass? She would be unable to live with herself if anything happened to him. Then Kathy had to think about the girl and her future. Kathy did not have a choice. She had to tell her brother the truth before it was too late. Kathy knew she shouldn't have kept this from Big Papa. Red had her believe it was for the best.

RED'S DEVIL'S

She remembered five years ago when she got a call from a man named Red, introducing himself as Big Papa's boss and family. He had an offer for her that would save her brother's life, and she would never have to work again. All he needed her to do was take care of the little girl. Keep her safe. Claim her as her own. She prayed about it then told her relatives she had gotten pregnant and had a baby. When they asked who the father was, she said the father was no longer in the picture. Only she and Red would know she was hiding her brother's baby and claiming her as her own.

AMBER

Amber was ready to put her plan into action so she could be rid of Red. She wanted her life back and not to have to worry about it. Recently she had been watching her surroundings more. She was afraid someone would come to try to snatch her right off the street and force her to become a devil, whether she wanted to or not. Amber was walking out of CVS,

RED'S DEVIL'S

picking up her mom's prescriptions, when Red pulled up on her in the parking lot.

"You are so damn beautiful. I can't keep living without you by my side." He said to Amber as she walked to her car.

"I have no interest in your club, Red. Why can't you leave me alone?"

"Come with me to Red Devil. Let me show you, and I promise I will leave you alone." He opened her door for her.

Amber climbed into her car and put the keys in the ignition. "If I come to your club, will you leave me alone? You are not the type to take no, for an answer; you are very persistent, Red. I will stop by and take a look. Then you will see that I'm persistent too. I say what I mean." "Ok, I will take that, Amber. I hope you change your mind. See you tonight."

"See you later, Red; I have high expectations." Amber pulled off, smiling to herself. Time to see what it was all about. Time to play Red's game.

RED'S DEVIL'S

Chapter 27

YIELDS

"I don't think going to Red Devil alone is a good idea. I should go with you. I don't trust Red." Ambers met his lips.

"Don't worry; I can manage Red. It's a public place. What can he do in a building full of witnesses?" Yields pulled Amber's clothes and kissed her forehead. "I still think I should be there. Those people in Red Devil are all Reds. They wouldn't be any help to you. Red does what he wants when he wants. There's some shit going down at Red Devil I don't want you involved in. I will explain later. Do you have your gun with you?"

Amber pulled her gun out of her purse and showed Yields. "Never leave home without it. I'm ready for Red." She checked her clip. It was fully loaded.

"Please be careful and don't stay too long. Keep texting me every few minutes, and if you don't respond, I'm coming in after you."

RED'S DEVIL'S

"Listen, I know you are worried, and I will text you back to let you know I'm Ok. Don't worry; I know how to manage your best friend. I will call you later tonight and tell you how it went."

Yields wasn't feeling the situation at all. He couldn't protect Amber if he wasn't there. He couldn't just show up and say he was looking for Amber. He had to play it cool. Then she could be rid of Red and Yields. Red had to be up to something. Whatever it was, he had not included Yields in it so Yields knew it could be nothing good. Amber should have never agreed to meet Red anywhere. He was too slick for his good. Yields couldn't help but feel like something was going down today, and he would not be able to see exactly what it was.

FRED

Red told Fred to escort Amber to his office as soon as she arrived. He told Fred to park her car in the private garage outback. Fred couldn't figure out what

RED'S DEVIL'S

Red had planned. He has been working for Red for over 15 years. He knew when the wheels were turning in his head. Fred had to be on his toes. Too much shit was happening at one time. A whole lot of bombs were about to explode. Fred was glad Lisa was gone for the night. This was her night recruiting females to join her family at Red Devil. Fred knew Lisa had been feeling some way about risky behavior with these females lately. He has been acting out of character for some time now. Something was going on with Red, something no one else knew but him.

Fred did as he was told. He parked Amber behind the business and Red's garage, then showed her to Red's office. He knocked on the door. Red told them to enter, and Fred closed the door behind him.

"I'm so glad you decided to give me a chance." Red stood up and walked over to Amber.

"You didn't give me a choice in this matter. I figured this way I could get you off my back."

Red sat on the corner of his desk. "Would you like a tour of Red Devil?" Red tried to touch Amber's hand, but she pulled away before he could. "I want you to

be comfortable here, Get familiar with the place and the people in it. This could be a place you call home."
Amber rolled her eyes.

"I'm in business for myself. I work for myself and answer to no one."

"That could change for the better. You can keep all your business and plenty more, just a few rules and the devil tattoo…."

Amber interrupted. Red. "Tattoo! What tattoo?" That took Amber by surprise.

"It's nothing too serious when you become a devil and join the family; you get a tattoo to show your loyalty and commitment to the family and me. All the girls have it. Your bank account won't complain about the tattoo. I need you here. You are the most beautiful woman I have seen in a long time. Give me the honor to go in business with you."

"As I said, Red, I'm doing fine alone. I have everything you are offering me. I'm stuck in my way. I don't do well with change. I'm sure you can relate with being a businessman and all." She went to walk toward the door, and he grabbed her by the arm.

RED'S DEVIL'S

"Before you leave, let me show you something that might interest you. I need a few more minutes of your time."

Red led her to the door to his toy box. He opened the door and let her into the toy box. Amber was dizzy from trying to see everything. It was like a sex store exploded in his big ass sex playpen. You could live any sexual fantasy that you could ever think of. What the fuck was going on in here behind these closed doors?

"This is my toy box. I love to play. Guess you can call me a kid at heart. Do you like to play Amber?" Red closed the door and locked it.

"I see you like to keep busy. I have my bag of tricks. I think I'm good. Thanks for the tour. But I have a prior engagement, so I think it's time for me to go."

Amber tried to reach for the doorknob, and Red grabbed her by her hair and threw her on the bed. She went to grab her gun, but it was in her purse on Red's desk in his office. Fuckin shit!! She was in trouble! Amber tussled with Red, but he ended up restraining both her arms and then her legs.

RED'S DEVIL'S

"What the fuck do you think you're doing? Let me go, Red! This isn't funny. I'm not about to play your sick games. Let me loose now!"

Red got a mouth gag to shut her up. Amber didn't know how the hell she was going to get out of this shit! Yields was her only hope. If she didn't send Yield a text, he said he would come for her. Amber prayed. He kept his word and came looking for her.

"Get comfortable, Amber, you will grow to love it here at Red Devils, and you will begin to see that we are a perfect match made in heaven, or should I say in hell. You're my beautiful little devil. I will be back soon." Amber was trying to scream through the gag, but it was no use. No one would hear her. What did Red have planned for her? Where the hell was Yields?

YIELDS

Yields kept calling and texting Amber, but he wasn't getting a response. He knew he should have stopped her from going there by herself or at all. Now he had to go and save Amber. He just had to figure out exactly how he would do that. He rushed to the Red Devil, jumped out of his car, ran right past Red, and went straight to Red's office. He didn't even knock. He burst right in. "Where's the fire? What have you got for me?" Red was smiling.

"Just was checking on things before I head in for the night." Yields was texting Amber's phone when the purse on Red's desk vibrated. Yields knew that it was Amber's purse. Red saw Yields was looking at the bag, and he grabbed it and stuffed it in his desk drawer.

"How did it go with Amber?"

"It went well; she will be joining the family. She had other engagements, so she left."

Yields knew that story was utterly untrue. He just saw Amber's purse, and he was sure her purse was vibrating. Which meant her phone was in her purse. So where was Amber? And why is he lying about it? He didn't see Amber's car outside in the parking lot. He didn't know what was going on, but he had to figure it out. Where was Amber? What had Red done? He knew Fred wouldn't be of any help. Yields knew Fred would die with Red's secrets. He checked the parking lot but there was no sign of Amber's car. If she left her phone behind, she left in a hurry. If she did leave, where the hell was, she? Yields was getting frustrated. He didn't know what to do; He felt helpless as hell. Amber needed his help, and he had no clue how to do that.

DARA

Dara had been a devil for a few weeks and so far, everything has been great. Excellent clients, good money, everything was great except for the part about her being stalked. She came out of her front door to find all four of her tires slashed. Dara instantly called Red. Whoever this creepy, creepy person was, they were going too far. Red sent a car to pick Dara up. He had her car towed, and all the tires replaced. Dara still had no clue who would be doing this to her and why. She didn't have any enemies that she knew of. Time for some of that protection Red was talking about.

RED'S DEVIL'S

The car shop found a GPS hidden under Dara's car. They called and told Red, and Red told Dara. Whoever this stalker was, he was serious.

Red moved Dara into one of his three-bedroom, two bathrooms houses, that he already had furnished. She had to sign the lease and pick up her keys. Dara was living and driving in luxury, making good money and getting good sex regularly. There seemed to be no limit of clients and the clients were drowning in money. It was plenty to go around and plenty of Red to go around as well. Dara didn't think she was ready to play second position in another man's life. Trevor was enough. Red didn't mind being with his devils, but Dara didn't think she could share Red with anyone, not even Lisa.

Chapter 28
LISA

Lisa was supposed to be out recruiting women for Red, not tonight. She has some business to take care of. Fred tried to warn her. He wanted to talk her out of trying to discover Red's secrets. If Freddie Bear hadn't helped her, that would have been fine with her. Lisa was too determined to find the truth, whether ugly or hurtful. Nothing was going to stop her on her quest for answers. Red would have no choice but to come clean. He would be unhappy with Lisa if he knew she was digging around in his private affairs. The way she was feeling right now, she didn't give a fuck about his feelings. What about her feelings? Who did he see in Paris? Was he hiding Naomi? Did they have something going on? Why hadn't Red told her about the properties in Paris? Why hadn't he taken her to Paris?

He knew that it was her dream to live in Paris. Every time Lisa brought up Paris, he would tell her they would move and retire to Paris once they had finished with Red Devils. He made that promise 15 years ago. All while, Red was going to Paris all along. Now she finds out he has property there in his mother's name. She's supposed to be his dead mother and supposedly died while he was a young child. That's how he ended up in foster care.

Not properly with his mother, the name is popping up. Yields didn't know what was going on. Was Red involved in some love affair with Naomi? Was he hiding her in Paris? Using his dead mother's name to hide Naomi? Lisa still needed to find her daughter. Then they could go to Paris together and be a family. She should have never listened to Red and given her baby up. Now she regretted it. She had to make things right; she had to find her daughter. Red didn't matter anymore. He made his decision. She still wanted to know who was in Paris and what he was doing there.

RED'S DEVIL'S

AMBER

Amber was bound and gagged in Red's toy box. No one knew where she was except for Red and Yields. What was taking him so long to come and save her? What if he knew Reds plan all along? Was he just going to hold her hostage until she agreed to become a devil? Did he think he could force her into giving in to him? How the hell would she get out of this shit? Why didn't she listen to Yields?? She didn't know if she could fully trust him. Now she was lying there wishing she had listened to Yields. How did she leave her damn purse on the desk? Amber was still trying to fight her way out of the restraints on her arm and legs, but it was useless. She was trapped with no way out.

RED

RED'S DEVIL'S

It was early morning when Red got to the Red Devils. He had to check on his newest Devil. If she wasn't ready, she had better get ready. There was no way he would let go of Amber now that he had her in his possession. Red was preparing himself. All the shit that was about to go down: he was ready to face anything. He was on Cloud 9, knowing behind that door was the woman of his dreams. He knew he had some hard decisions to make. Red knew what Lisa was up to. He knew what the outcome would look like. Was he really about to replace his number one? Red wasn't sure if it would be as easy as he had hoped, especially with Lisa hell bent on finding her daughter. He promised her that he would never hurt her. Real man, make your panties wet. Not your eyes. That was something Red always told Lisa. She was about to find out which one Red was.

YIELDS

RED'S DEVIL'S

Yields drove to Amber's house; there was no sign of her car, and the place was utterly dark. It didn't make sense to call her phone since it was in her purse on Red's desk back at Red Devil. Then he remembered the tracking device he put on Amber's car. According to the GPS, Amber's car was at Red Devil. It had to be in Red's garage. That meant Amber never left.

Where the hell was she? He had to go back to the Red Devil, and he needed to get into Red's office alone. That was not going to be so easy. The only place she could be is in the toy box. What was Red doing in there? Did she decide to give in to Red and become a devil? Was she switching up on him and choosing Red over him? What was going on? Yields needed to know if he had lost Amber to Red.

Why did Red always get the girl? Yields were fed up with living in Red's shadow. He followed his rules and was loyal to him. Risking his career and sometimes his life for Red He had been Red's clean-up man for almost 20 long years. Enough was enough; he would not give in to Red this time. Amber was his soul mate. They were meant to be together, and Red was in the way of his happiness. Red already has everything he could want. Now he wanted Amber. It wouldn't matter if he told Red how he felt about Amber. Red wouldn't give a damn. He would throw money at Yields and tell him to find another girl. One that Red had no interest in.

He needed to contact Arab. Maybe he could get help solving his problem by helping Arab find Naomi and discover the truth about her being a devil and Red helping her escape from him. Arab could then deal with it while he and Amber ran away together and be rid of Red. Whatever he was going to do, he needed to do it fast. He didn't know how much time he had, but he had to save Amber.

RED

Red went into his toy box and removed the mouth gag and the restraints. Amber jumped off the bed and charged at Red, ready to throw down.

RED'S DEVIL'S

"Calm down, Amber—no need for violence. I thought you needed some time alone to think things over. To help you come to a healthy decision about joining my family." Amber slapped Red, then hit him again. Red grabbed both her arms, pinned them over her head, and pushed her against the mirror. Then he gave her a long, deep kiss. She bit his lip and tasted blood in her mouth. She was ready to kill Red. If only she had her damn purse with her gun in it.

"Let me out of here right now, damn it! You think locking me up, holding me against my will, will change my mind! Are you fucking serious?! Let me out of here and now! Let me get out of here and now!" She ran for the door.

"It's no use, the door is locked, and I have the key. If you give me some time, you will see how wonderful Red Devils is. You will grow to like it." Red watched Amber pull and push on the door.

She was outraged, pissed, dehydrated, and hungry. Amber wanted out of the toy box. She couldn't believe Red. He had some serious issues. The man was flat-out crazy! If she managed to get out of there, she might have to take Yields up on his offer about leaving town or even faking her death. Red wasn't going to be easy to deal with, as she thought.

"You can stay here a bit longer if you need more time, or you can fill out these papers, get your tattoo and start your new life at Red Devils."

He picked up a whip and said, " If you still want to be a bad girl, I could punish you. Then you can return the favor." Red licked his lips.

"I'm never going to be a devil. So, you're going to hold me here forever?" She sat down on the bed. She didn't see any opportunity to get out of that damn room. There was no way out unless she agreed to be a devil. If that's what she had to do to get out of that room, then so be it. "OK, fine, I will join your family and be a devil. I will sign the papers. Just tell me what I need to do." Red had a big, satisfying smile on his face.

"I'm so glad you came to your senses. I knew you were just as bright as you are beautiful. Happy to have you in the family. Come on, let's get this done.

RED'S DEVIL'S

I'm sure you want to go shower and get yourself together."

Red unlocked the door, and they both walked into Red's office. He locked the entrance to the toy box and put the key in his pocket. They both sat down, and Red gave Amber the forms to fill out and his list of house rules. "Are you serious about these rules? Do you want me to get a tattoo branded like some cattle? I don't like the idea of that at all." She dropped the ink pen on the desk.

"I'm afraid I have to disagree with all this. If you want me here so badly, we will have to compromise with one another. According to you, I'm not like the other women here. And if that's true, I shouldn't have to follow the same rules as everyone else. You said to get comfortable, so I'm telling you what. It will and won't make me comfortable. I'm tired, and I want to go home. I will call you shortly; now, give me my damn purse so I can get out of here. I have shit to do."

Red took her wallet out of his desk and handed it to her. Then he called Fred and had him escort Amber to her car. Red had his prize. He felt like a king in his castle, surrounded by beautiful women. Now he had the most beautiful woman in West Virginia. Red had big plans for Amber, plans he knew Lisa was not going to agree with.

FRED

Fred had never seen Red like this before, holding Amber against her will like that so he could bring her into the Red Devil. Fred was beginning to get very worried about the whole situation. How did Red expect all this to play out? Freddy's main focus was to keep Lisa safe. Telling her the truth might be the best thing he could do for her, even if it meant losing her forever. He did not want to harm Lisa and if she found out about her daughter, life as they knew it would be over. Why should he stand in the way of her finding her child? Why continue to help Red hurt Lisa? He knew how hurt Lisa was when she gave up her daughter. All because of Red. Now he was trying to keep her from reuniting with her daughter. Fred carried that guilt around with him every day for 15 years. Fred thought it was time to set Lisa free. Free from Red Devil, free from Red and all his lies and bullshit

Nothing would make Fred happier than seeing Lisa genuinely happy for a change. She tried to walk around and pretend like she was good with everything, but she was hurting deep inside. Lisa was like a chameleon; she could adapt to any situation. She had learned a lot from reading over the years. Lisa was no dummy; she was street-smart and book smart. Red made sure of that. He put a lot of work into grooming Lisa. Now she would take everything he taught her and use it against him if she had to. Fred knew Lisa well enough to know that eventually she would have all her answers, and then she would find her daughter.

Chapter 29

AMBER

When Amber pulled up to the house, she saw Yields parked out front.

"Oh my God! Are you OK? What happened? Where were you? Did he hurt you?" Yields were examining Amber, checking her over.

"Calm down; I'm OK. I will be better once I shower, eat, and sleep." They both walked into Amber's house.

"I came looking for you when you didn't answer my text. Red told me you had left, but I saw your purse on his desk. There was no way for me to have gotten you out without having to shoot my way in. That would not have been pretty." Amber was getting undressed. She went into the bathroom and turned on her shower.

"I can't believe he held me hostage in his motherfucking sex dungeon until I agreed to be a devil and join his family! He thinks I will let him brand me with some devil tattoo.! He had me strapped to a mother fucking bed and gagged! He's a freaking psycho! How could you be friends with such a crazy, Ruthless man? It's something very wrong with him." Yields was watching Amber's every move.

Everything she did was so feminine and sexy. Amber was sexy without even trying. Yields was falling increasingly in love with Amber if that was possible. Amber was very aware that Yields was watching her. She slowly walked into the bathroom completely naked and showered. Yields were sitting there, dick hard as a rock. He was imagining the smell of her skin and wondered how soft her skin felt. Yields went into the bathroom and stood in the doorway momentarily, watching her silhouette under the warm water. Her body was soaking wet. Yields open the shower door.

"I thought you might need some help."

Amber looked so good that he could not resist her any longer. He stepped out of his shoes, dropped his pants and underwear, then removed his shirt. Amber didn't say anything; She just watched him watch her. Yields stepped into the shower with Amber and pulled her face up to him. He pushed her wet hair from her face and gently kissed her. The kiss was so passionate it sent a chill through her whole body. He caressed her body, feeling her skin, learning all the curves of her beautiful body. He rubbed her breast then he licked her shoulders, softly kissed her neck, and nibbled on her ear.

He picked her up and slid right in her wet hot pussy. Amber let out a soft moan of pleasure. She could not believe what she was doing. This was not part of the plan. The water was still running down both of their bodies. His thrusts began to go deeper and faster. He couldn't get enough of her, and she felt like heaven. He never wanted to stop; She dug her nails into his back. Then she bit down on his shoulder. He carried her to the bedroom and laid her on the bed. He kissed her lips, her neck, her titties then her belly. He slid down to her pussy and slid his tongue inside; she was hot and wet, ready for more? He flipped her over and ate her out from the back until she came on his face. Then he slid back inside her. She gripped the sheets and bit down on the pillow to muffle her screams of pleasure. He rubbed her ass the smacked her in one good time. He pulled out and sucked, kissed, and licked her pussy again. Her body started gyrating back and forth; He knew she was about to climax, so he came with her.

    Amber thought she would never be with a white guy intimately ever again. Yields did something to her that made her fall for him. She didn't know exactly what it was about him, but it was something. She surprised herself. This was not supposed to happen. She should not be falling for this man. Red's best friend was just supposed to be a pawn in her game now, things were getting even more out of control. She had to figure out how to manage Red and what she would do about Yields. It was bad enough that she was starting to fall for him, even worse that Amber was starting to believe that Yields was really in love with her. All the things he said to her, he meant.

Could she see herself being with Yields? Leaving the country to start fresh with Yields? Could she give up her life and business and walk away for good, or would she be a devil? Could she disappear? Would she go by herself, or would she take Yields with her? First, she had to return to Red Devil and deal with Red. He would not get away with what he did to her that easily. Amber would never forgive nor forget what Red did.

Yields knew he would need Arab. Getting rid of Red was the only way he could have Amber to himself. Red didn't love Amber; he just liked to control people. Amber was like a prize to Red, like he won some contest. Sooner or later, he would get bored with her and find someone even prettier, he would forget all about Amber. He was just a selfish, greedy man. Yields had known that most of his life, Red had not changed and likely wouldn't any time soon. Yields knew that for sure. He used to love Red and had mad respect for him now all he felt was hate, envy, and jealousy. Yields was going to be the winner. Amber was his and his alone. Red won't be getting his girl. It was time for him to be the loser. He needed to learn how it feels not to get his way all the time. He had to choose Amber over his best friend. Red made that decision easy for him to make. He wished he didn't have to end like this, but it was the only option.

BIG PAPA

Big Papa received a phone call from his sister, Kathy early in the morning before he left for work at the Red Devil.

"Listen, I need you to hear me out and consider that I'm your sister, and it's my job to look out for you as much as possible. What I'm about to tell you will seem unbelievable and overwhelming. Just promise you will try to see things from my point of view. Do you think you can do that for me, brother??" Kathy was scared of Big Papa's reaction.

How would their relationship suffer from this big secret? Red's big secret.

"Sis, just spit it out. I know you love me, and you've been looking out for me all my life. What's wrong? It can't be that bad. I promise I will listen and try to see things from your point of view."

"I don't know where to start…."

"Just start from the beginning, I guess."

"OK, well, five years ago, I received a call from Red telling me he needed my help with something that would keep you out of danger. He told me about Naomi and her brother Arab. He said he had to get Naomi out of the country, and you couldn't know about it for your good. Then he came here with the baby girl. My baby girl. I was supposed to tell the family I was pregnant and had a daughter, your niece. The thing is, I was never pregnant. Naomi was pregnant, and Red asked me to take care of the baby

RED'S DEVIL'S

as if she was my own and keep his secret. He would pay me monthly to raise the baby—your niece. I mean, your daughter, your niece is your daughter. But I don't know where Naomi is, and I never knew. I was told that she was safe and alive. Red said he would never contact me again. I never heard from him in the five years, only his monthly checks. That was the arrangement. Arab would never know, and you would be safe, and so would your daughter. Then you start asking about Naomi and the two properties here in Paris under Red's dead mother's name. I'm unsure, but he's hiding Naomi in one of them. Now Arab is asking questions about Naomi, trying to find her. He would surely kill you if he ever learned about you, especially if he learned about the baby. He would try and take the baby away from Naomi. Then away from me. We are safe for now. Red paid for me to move to another place in Paris, France. I am worried about you and what's going to happen. Please don't hate me. I did it for you to save you, to protect you. I didn't have a choice." Kathy began to cry on the other end of the phone.

RED'S DEVIL'S

Big Papa sat on the edge of his bed, speechless. He could not believe what his sister had just said. All this time, five years. She kept this from him for five years! Knowing how he felt about Naomi., and how he was worried. How sad he was without her. Now she tells him that they have a daughter. That his sister has been posing his daughter as his niece. That shit robbed him of the bond and relationship with his daughter. He was trying to wrap his head around all of it. All he could do was shake his head and rub his face. He had a daughter. He and Naomi's little girl was five years old and living in Paris. If Red was responsible, he had to know where Naomi was.

Big Papa still could not find any words after hearing what he had just heard. He just hung the phone up and sat there staring at the walls. His mind was racing. He felt his blood pressure rising and thought he would have a damn heart attack. He has a daughter. A baby girl is living in Paris—a daughter with the only woman he ever loved. Naomi was still missing. If his sister didn't want him to hate her, she better help him find the mother of his child. Then maybe, just maybe, he could forgive Kathy. Right now, his focus is on finding Naomi. He needed to talk to Lisa as soon as possible.

DARA

Dara had a hard time falling asleep. She was too worried about her stalker. What would stop him from finding her again if he found her once? She decided to take a few shots of Hennessy to help her relax. She loved her new place, but she was still nervous. What if her stalker was outside right now? What if he followed her from work or the store or anywhere?

Dara finally dozed off when a noise woke her up. Dara sat up suddenly and grabbed her pepper spray from under her pillow. She walked out to the dining room, and there were two wine glasses on the table with some roses and chocolates and the CD player was playing soft music. Dara heard the floor creak behind her. When she turned around, she saw Trevor standing there with handcuffs.

RED'S DEVIL'S

Dara screamed "What the hell are you doing here? How did you get in? How do you know where I live? Have you been the one stalking me all this time? You slashed my fucking tires! Are you stupid or something?" Dara was so mad she was shaking.

"I'm the one that should be asking the damn questions! Do you think you can walk away from me that easily? You don't tell me it's over; I say when it's over! You are turning tricks now. That's what you're doing now? Some cheap bitch? You belong to me!" Trevor walked towards Dara, and she started backing up slowly.

"What are you doing, Trevor? Why are you here? Don't you have a wife? Should you be home with me? What is wrong with you? Why are you doing this?" Trevor was still walking toward her with the handcuffs." I told you; no one leaves me. You belong to me. I made you! You are mine and mine only!"

Dara tried to spray him with the pepper spray, but he charged at her too fast, and she dropped the pepper spray on the floor. They were both on the floor, scrambling for the pepper spray. Trevor knocked it out of her reach, and Dara screamed. Trevor put his hand over her mouth so no one would hear her. She knew no one was coming to save her period. Dara didn't know what Trevor intended to do too. They started tussling knocking over lamps and pictures. They fell on the floor, and he pinned her down. He tried to kiss Dara, but she kept turning her face. Then she spat in Trevor's face, so he slapped her. He ripped Dara's nightgown, trying to force her legs open. Dara tried to fight him off. Nothing she did stopped him from trying to take what he thought was his. "I licked it, so it's mine!" Trevor yelled and bit down on Dara's breast. She was screaming in pain as he flipped her over, pushed her hands back, and put the cuffs on her. He bent her over and started ramming his dick in her. He pushed her face down on the cushion while she was screaming from the pain. He was violating her in every way. Dara wanted to kill Trevor. She had never needed a weapon before. What could she do with her hands cuffed behind her back? Dara had to play along with him so that he would uncuff her.

RED'S DEVIL'S

"Stop, baby, Stop! Be gentle, daddy. You are right. I belong to you. I'm yours. Let me show you. Let me please you. Take these cuffs off and let me show you how much I love you." She was trying her best to convince him that she was serious.

"Now you going to show me whom this belongs to? No more hoeing around. You ready to be a good girl now?" He gladly uncuffed her, expecting her to show her appreciation to him. Darla stood up and started rubbing Trevor's chest and arms. Then she grabbed hold of his dick and squeezed it. Then she kneed him and his nuts and scratched his face. She took off running to the bedroom and closed and locked the door. She grabbed her cell phone and called Red.

"I called the police. They are on their way; you better get out of here now, Trevor!" Dara yelled through her bedroom door. Trevor ran out the front door and down the street to his parked car. He was trying to get out of there before the police came. If she called them, he wasn't worried. He would tell the police the sex was consensual, and she got upset because he didn't want to leave his wife for her, so she attacked him. It was his word over an angry, bitter ex-girlfriend.

Dara didn't call the police, she called Red, and he sent Fred to pick her up. She was shaken up and had a few bumps and bruises. As soon as Fred saw Dara, he knew what had happened to her. He hugged and held her tight, and tears poured down her face. She held on to Fred for dear life. She could not believe she had just been raped by the man she used to worship, a man she thought she would spend the rest of her life with. He was stalking her. He was harassing her and now just raped her in her house. She can't let him get away with that shit. If he ever came near her again, she would kill him. Red promised to take her to the firing range and teach her how to use a gun. She was more than ready to learn. Trevor had better stay far the fuck away from her because she would be ready the next time.

LISA

RED'S DEVIL'S

Lisa walked and arrived at the office like she always did, and she went to open the door to the toy box, but her key didn't work. So, she started rummaging through Red's desk.

He walked in and said. "Looking for something sexy?" He dangled a set of keys in the air. "Why won't my key work? When did you change the locks? And why did you change the locks?"

"Don't worry, my love. I'm having some work done in there. I don't want anyone in there until it's done. Please respect my privacy for now. Can you do that for me, my love?" Lisa was sick of all the bullshit.

"Respect your privacy! Are you fucking serious right now? Privacy, Red! Like your monthly trips? I will give you your privacy. With all the women, I give you your privacy—all your shady business deals. I provide you with privacy!"

"Fuck you, Red. And fuck this mutherfucker! Why the fuck are you going to Paris every month for a week for the last 15 years!" Lisa was screaming at the top of her lungs. Red just sat there like a statue, letting Lisa rant and rave.

RED'S DEVIL'S

"Are you finished yet, my dear?"

Lisa picked up a paperweight, threw it at the mirror, and shattered it." Tell me about Paris, Red. Tell me now and tell me everything, or else I'm walking out the door for good!" She was serious as hell.

"Again, I need you to respect my privacy. I will explain what you need to know when the time is right. For now, we have bigger things to worry about. I know you and Big Papa have uncovered some things about Naomi. Yes, I helped her disappear to save her from her brother. I had to protect Big Papa, you know, he's family. Can you let me manage things? And when it's all said and done, I will tell you anything you want to know."

"Why couldn't you tell Big Papa what was happening? Having him depressed for five years, wondering where she was and if she was alive? How could you do that to your own family?"

"I had to. It was the only way to keep him from Arab's wrath of fury. Arab is my problem, and I will handle him. Now can we please move forward with our day?" He kissed Lisa's forehead, nose, and hands.

RED'S DEVIL'S

"I'm serious, Red. I want to know everything. When this shit is over, you will help me find our daughter!" Lisa stormed out of the office and went to see Big Papa.

BRITTANY

Brittany walked past Lisa, storming out of Red's office. Lisa stopped and told Brittany.

"You don't belong here. You better leave while you can." Then she walked off singing. Brittany didn't pay Lisa, any mind she had to see Red.

"You don't know how happy I am to see you Bold Brittany." Red clapped his hands together. "Nice to see you, Red; we need to talk." Red started unbuttoning his shirt.

"What are you waiting for? I need to talk to you as well, I think better when you're naked." Brittany grabbed his hands.

"Red, I said we need to talk."

RED'S DEVIL'S

Red tried to unzip Britney's jacket. "Take these clothes off, and I'll talk to you all night if you like." Brittany pushed Red back. He thought they were going to play rough. Just how he liked it. "Red, I made up my mind. I won't be joining your little clan of devils. It was fun, it was a lot of fun, but this is not for me. I don't do drama, secrets, or lies. And I will never compete with another woman. So, I won't be signing any forms or getting your little devil branded on me, either. I was going through some stuff and let things get out of hand. I let things go too far. I'm not that kind of person. I'm not who you think I am. I'm too old to play high school games and I don't like to share. Call me selfish or stubborn. That's just how it is. You have your hands full already. There is no room for me here. I'm sure your devils love you, and they are happy. That's the difference between your devils and me. I don't need a man to control me. I do fine by myself. Goodbye, Red. Enjoy your night." Before Red could get a word out, Brittany was gone.

She felt better now. She had to remove herself from that whole situation. It was time to snap out of it

RED'S DEVIL'S

and get back to reality. Back to her reality, which did not include Red or anything to do with the Red Devil. While Fred walked her to the parking lot to her car. Some fine ass man approached Brittany. She smelled his Nautica Cologne as he approached her.

"Hello Fred. How have you been doing?" They shook hands and greeted each other.

"Hello Miss, you are gorgeous." He smiled at Brittany.

"Thank you." Britney smiled.

They were checking each other out. Brittany liked what she saw. This man was sexy as hell. He looked like he had just left a business meeting.

"Don't tell me I'm too late. You're leaving already?"

"Yes, I'm leaving. I don't work here. I was passing through."

"People say Red has the most beautiful woman in the state dancing here. I must say, seeing you makes me a believer. It's a shame you're leaving. I want to buy you a drink and learn more about you. If that's possible."

RED'S DEVIL'S

"You could buy me a drink, but not here and not tonight. Can I have a rain check?" Brittany pulled out her cell phone.

"Put my number on your phone and call me tomorrow when you are free. I'm Brittany. Nice to meet you."

"I'm Jovon, but my friends call me Joe." He pulled his phone out and programmed Brittany's number into his phone.

Today must have been his lucky day. He came right at the perfect time to meet this sexy young lady. Fred just smiled and walked back into the club. Fred had known Jovon for a few years. He knew Brittany would be safe with Jovon. He was like a regular at the Red Devil.

Jovan was an engineer, 45 years old, with a daughter and an ex-wife. Jovan was handsome and very wealthy. He loved his fame and fortune. Jovan was a brilliant man. Jovan was an engineer, and he did his job very well. He had money and wasn't afraid to spend it. He only had a few tattoos and wore two diamond rings in his ear. He didn't smoke cigarettes, but he smoked a blunt every once in a while. Jovon

RED'S DEVIL'S

was a mechanical engineer. He designed, made, installed and fixed power-producing machines like generators, engines, and medical equipment.

Jovan had come a long way from slanging on corners, stealing cars, and riding around in his 85 Jeep Cherokee, to driving his Ferrari and having his private jet and properties around the world. He had a shit load of money with the lips to go along with it. Jovon was a businessman and a good father. He had his only daughter when he was 25 years old. That's what made him change his life and become successful at what he did. He ensured his parents were well taken care of, and his daughter was as well. He lived in Florida but had property on the West Coast of Africa. He would never have imagined coming this far and not graduating high school. He got his GED and did some college. Then he began his career. Over the years, Jovan has lost close childhood friends to murder, suicide, and overdose. Jovon loved his life. He loved making money. When it came to money, he could never have enough. He wouldn't have a problem with spending it on Brittany.

RED'S DEVIL'S

JOVON

Jovon had been in Africa for the last six months. He decided to return to the States, visit Red Devil, catch up with an old friend, and see beautiful devils. Jovon was glad he made the trip, or he would have never met Brittany. She was lovely to Jovon. He could see her by his side. He would try to make that happen the first chance he got. He use to date a stripper in Cleveland, but it did not work out so currently he was single. It might not have been in his best interest to date another stripper, but something about Brittany pushed all the doubt to the back of his mind. He would have to call Brittany; He wanted to know everything about her.

LISA

RED'S DEVIL'S

Detective Yields was sitting in the dining area by the kitchen, and she walked right past him. Lisa had to talk to Big Papa. He told her about Red helping Naomi disappear and about their baby living in Paris with his sister for five years. His sister found the properties in Red's name, and they still did not know where Naomi was, and Red wasn't giving up any information. Big Papa knew his life could be at risk.

Yields was eavesdropping on their conversation. Lisa and Big Papa didn't even notice him listening. He needed something to give Arab so they could eliminate their problem. Lisa had to know the whole story. Lisa thought she was getting close to figuring it all out. She didn't care if Arab knew the truth as long as she found her daughter. Right now, she could care less what happened to Red between him and Arab as long as she wasn't impaired. If anybody were going to kill her husband though, it would be her.

JOVON

RED'S DEVIL'S

Jovon hadn't been to the Red Devil in a few months. He didn't know that Red Hot Dara was a new devil trying to get Amber and Brittany to become devils. Jovon knew he was very interested in getting to know Brittany more intimately. Jovon went into Red's office to catch up. They had a shot of Hennessy and fell in on Daring Dara; then Red told Jovon how he was recruiting Britney. That caught Jovon's attention. He realized Brittany was not a devil, at least not yet. He had a chance, after all. Jovon wanted his chance with Brittany without any complications. Jovon didn't look at risk as competition, so Jovon said to Red. "Let the best man win." Jovon had every intention of winning. He was not a gambling man; Red was. He was convinced that he had what it took to make a woman love him without exploiting or bullying her like Red dealt with his devils. Jovon believed in seizing the moment. Brittany did not belong to Red just yet. Jovon planned on keeping it that way.

They finished a bottle of Hennessy before Jovon left.

RED'S DEVIL'S

"I hope you're ready because I don't take no for an answer." Red says to Jovon.

"I don't play games. I will win!" Jovon said to Red, then left Red's office with a smile.

RED

"Get some of your guys. I have a job for you. I need a package picked up and delivered. Be gentle with the cargo. This package is essential; Please handle it with care. I'm guessing you can manage that. Bring the package here straight to me. Use the back entrance. I will cut the cameras off in the back until you have them deliver the package." He wrote down the address on a slip of paper and handed it to Fred. He handed him a needle.

"You will be needing this as well." Red handed Fred the syringe.

"Red, Are you sure about this? I know you go after what you want, but this... Don't you think this is going a little too far?"

RED'S DEVIL'S

"I don't remember asking for your opinion."

"I don't remember signing up for this sick shit either!" Fred was pissed.

"Listen, I'm sorry. If there were any other way, I would have done it. This will be the last time I ask you to do something like this. If he's there when you are, and your team gets there, don't kill him; just rough him up. Is it safe to say that no one will be able to identify you?" Red knew Fred was an expert on missions like this. Fred was a professional.

"Fred, once this is done, there is no going back."

"That's exactly why I'm doing it." Red smiled an evil villain smile. Fred shook his head. He did not want to do this. It was no way he could disobey Red's wishes. He could not count how often he had gone against his beliefs doing shit for Red or cleaning up his messes. All the shit that detective Yields couldn't manage Fred has been handling for the last 15 years.

Fred thought to himself; it was time to move on. He was too old for this shit. He could live off his savings, he was financially set for life. He only stayed at the Red Devil long as he had because it gave him purpose. He felt useful. It kept him busy doing something he enjoyed, protecting people. Now it seemed like he was going down a dark path, and Red was leading him there

"Do this for me and it will be the last time, I mean it! I love you like a brother, but I won't turn into something I don't recognize when I look in the mirror daily."

"I'm tired of living with your lies and covering up your secrets. It's exhausting." Fred put the syringe in his pocket, and left Red's office. Red said out loud, talking to himself. "Once I have my package, I won't need anything else.

LISA

Lisa had a job to do. Get Dara back on track. Make her feel safe again. So, she took Dara to the shooting range to learn how to shoot a 9-millimeter

"Look, not to be in your business, but Freddie Bear, I mean, Fred told me what happened to you. That was real fucked up. You need to kill his ass, or he will do it again, trust me, I know. This gun right here will give you your power. Do you feel me? What's his name? Timothy?" Dara shook her head and whispered." Trevor". It took everything in her to say his name out loud.

"You will be ready for Trevor next time that stalking freak tries anything with you; just empty the clip."

"What does that mean?

"Keep pulling the trigger until you're out of bullets." Lisa picked up her silver-plated 9-millimeter and emptied her clip into the target. She did not miss, not one time.

"See. It feels good; It's simple. I've been shooting since I was 15 years old. Red and Fred used to bring me here all the time. I'm in the business so you have to be prepared to protect yourself. If you have a weapon, you have to know how to use it."

Dara picked up her gun, put on her headphones, and started firing. She knew it would be long before she could be as good as Lisa. As long as she hits whatever target she's aiming at, preferably Trevor.

RED'S DEVIL'S

"What's the deal with you and Red? Are you all like swingers or something?" Dara wasn't trying to be smart, she just really wanted to know.

"You could say something like that." Lisa shrugged her shoulders. She was not about to discuss Red with one of his new play toys.

"You don't have to talk about it. I was being nosy; I should have kept my mouth shut."

"You good, we are partners, and we run a business together, Let's just leave it at that." Lisa put her headphones on again, and she started singing and shooting. Dark kept practicing; She was a good shot. Lisa thought Dara could manage herself with a little more practice. Trevor better watches his back.

BRITTANY

Brittany was at EBO's, ordering some catfish and fries when she ran into Lisa.

RED'S DEVIL'S

"Hey Brittany, are you still deciding? Did you fall under Red's spell like all the other devils?" Lisa ate a fry.

"Sorry to disappoint. I had to turn him down." Brittany paid for her food.

"Being a devil can change your life. This isn't just some dive bar like these other clubs, The Red Devil is classy. The women are elegant. The club is refined." Lisa really could care less if Britney stayed or not. She was going through the motions.

"At The Red Devil, if any man breaks just one of the rules he's permanently out, we don't deal with thugs and gangsters. These are grown men, sophisticated, intelligent, hardworking businesspeople. They are all worth buckets of money that they don't mind emptying into our bank accounts. There are six rules a man can never break in here. The first rule is he should never ask for change for a 5. The second rule is he can never ask you for your real name. The third rule is he can never offer to take you out as a tip. The fourth rule is he cannot ask you to hook him up with one of the other females. The fifth rule is if he says he's only coming for a beer, and the last rule is, he cannot ask to get VIP treatment. If you hear any of these statements inside Red Devil, they don't belong here, and we must be doing poorly. Our client list is very exclusive. It would be worth the money with so little effort. These men come from beauty., mystery, and fantasy. That's what we provide. I'm sure you wouldn't regret it."

Brittany got her change and headed to the door. "That sounds good and all, but I'm not devil material. I told Red I was not interested." Brittany walked to her car.

"You looked highly interested the other night." Lisa walked across the street, entered her red Jaguar, and drove off. Brittany sat in her car for a moment, trying to figure out what Lisa's agenda was. Why was she so adamant about Brittany becoming a devil? What would she get out of it? Is she working on a commission or something? Lisa received a cut for each devil she tricked into becoming the devil.

Brittany promised herself she would not return to The Red Devil for any reason until she met Jovon.

RED'S DEVIL'S

Meeting Jovon might give her a reason to go to The Red Devil. She knew Red would not be too happy to see her with Jovon, his good longtime friend. Did Brittany have something planned? Will she design the jealousy game and break up the friendship? What is it she wanted?

AMBER

Detective Yields cooked dinner for him and Amber at her place. They were enjoying dinner and drinking a bottle of Hennessy. They made love three times, and it was like he could not get enough of Amber. She felt herself falling for him, and that was not part of the plan. Yields was sitting on the couch watching Amber in the kitchen, fixing them some drinks when the front door was kicked in. Four men in army fatigue and with war paint on their face stormed the room. Before Yields could get off the couch, he was jumped by two of the unknown men, and the other men grabbed Amber and threw her to the floor.

RED'S DEVIL'S

"He said not to hurt her!" One of the intruders said. The first iron man hit Yields in the back of the head. He was knocked out cold. The man grabbed her arms and legs while the other man pulled a syringe from his pocket and stuck it in Amber's neck. She was out before he even pulled the needle out of her neck. They left Yields unconscious on the floor, took Amber outside, put her in the back of the van, and drove off.

BIG PAPA

Big Papa could not tell Arab about him, Naomi, or their daughter living in Paris or about Red's properties in his mother's name in Paris. He would be putting his family and the woman he loved in danger. He had to devise something to hold Arab off until he could find an army. Then he would have to figure out how to save himself, Naomi, and his daughter from an evil, vengeful man.

RED'S DEVIL'S

FRED

Fred pulled the van up in the back of Red Devil, and carried Amber in. Only two other people knew about the secret passage from Red's office to the outside garage in the back of the building. Fred carried Amber into the toy box and placed her gently on the bed.

"That will be all. Here's your money for you and your men. I have everything under control from here."

Red tossed a duffel bag full of money at Fred's feet. Fred picked up the bag and left without saying a word. He did not feel right. He should have tried harder to talk Red out of this ridiculous plan; nor should he have gotten his war buddies involved. They were mercenaries, so it was just a job to them. They accept the mission, carry it out, and get paid, no questions asked. Fred was a little more connected to the situation, he and Red had history. An exceptionally long history. Fred was ready to retire and become a motivational speaker. To reach out and truly help people by positively lifting them up. He was tired of living on the dark side and breaking his conduct rules for money. It was time to get out of Red's clutches once and for all. He felt he had wasted enough years being a bad guy. He was following Reds orders and his rules. He needed to separate himself from the Red Devil and Reds Devils altogether. He wondered if he was strong enough to walk away from Lisa.

YIELDS

Yields woke up with a splitting headache, a black eye, and a busted nose. They worked him over. He was still a little bit dizzy. His head was spinning, and he saw stars. The place was trashed, and Amber was gone. This was indeed the work of Red. He had taken things too damn far this time. They should not have left him alive. Now he was on a mission to save Amber and end this shit. No more game-playing. Red has to go.

RED'S DEVIL'S

AMBER

Amber woke up and gagged. Her vision was still a little foggy. As she was coming out the fog she knew exactly where she was, back in the toy box. Red has crossed the line, big time. He had her kidnapped. What did he plan to do? Keep her hostage for the rest of her life? Did he hurt Yields? Was he in on this? This time she did not fight the restraints; she just waited for Red to show his face.

The door to the toy box opened, and Red walked in with a tray of food he had Big Papa prepared and some bottled water. He took the gag from her mouth and untied her. She spat right in Red's face. He wiped it off with the back of his hand.

"A little aggressive, aren't you? Don't worry; the worst part is over. You are home. I hope it's to your liking my newest devil. You are so damn beautiful. Now you're all mine." Red left the tray of food and clothes and locked the door behind him. Amber was trapped again, with no way out, and no one knew where she was. No one except Yields. This felt like Déjà vu. She began to doubt that Yields would be able to save her. Did Red expect her to stay locked up in his toy box until she gave in? Did he think he was in some movie? Amber had to figure out how to escape.

ARAB

Arab met Lisa at the Italian restaurant directly across the street from EBO's Restaurant.

"So, I have information for you, but I need your word about something. I tell you what you need to know, and no one gets hurt. You get your sister and go. Forget about everything else."

"From the sound of it, you know where Naomi is." He crossed his arms.

"Not quite yet, but I'm close; give me a few days and promise you won't hurt Big Papa or Fred, and I will get your sister back." Lisa hoped he would agree.

RED'S DEVIL'S

"You didn't mention your partner in crime Red."

"He is no concern of mine."

Lisa left the restaurant, leaving Arab to think about her offer. Would he forget Red's betrayal and walk away with Naomi? Arab made people disappear for less. As Red said, a bitch is replaceable, but a queen is not. Lisa was indeed a queen, not Red's queen anymore. This queen was ready to find her little Princess, Lisa May. She wanted a king, but she could run her castle alone. She had built a small dynasty for herself. She secured financial stability for her future. Once she had her daughter back. And she knew Big Papa and Freddy Bear would say she would leave Red Devil for good, with or without him. He could deal with Arab on his own. She was done playing his mind games. It was time to break free from all of it. Go to Paris, France just like she had been planning for so long.

Arab wanted Naomi back, but he wasn't sure he was in such the mood to forgive the lies and betrayal. Arab was a man of his word. He gave Red a promise that there would be severe consequences if he broke his rule. Now Lisa wants Arab to turn the other cheek. He didn't have to agree with Lisa. There were ways he could make her talk and still make everyone involved pay. Would he keep his word or let this one incident slide? Would Red get a free pass? What about Naomi, baby? What would happen to her? Then he will find out about Big Papa's involvement with Naomi. Who knows how Arab would react to the news? Did Lisa think she could manage the outcome of her actions? Lisa was 100% devoted to Red, but now she doesn't even know who he was anymore or what he was doing. Arab thought he would see what Lisa had to say in a few more days until he could be reunited with his sister. His most valuable possession. One he was not willing to give up on. He could tell her what she wanted to hear and do whatever she wanted.

YIELDS

RED'S DEVIL'S

He knew precisely where Amber was. Playtime is over. He had to get Amber as far away from Red as possible. He was beginning to lose his mind. He finally cracked, the power and money had consumed him. He has taken things entirely too far. He acted like he was a god, and everyone was here to serve him. Yields planned on bringing him back to reality. It was time for Red to live in the real world with actual rules and consequences. Time for Red to learn a lesson. He needed a reality check. Yields would be sure Red did just that; learned his lesson. There is such a word as No. Red couldn't have everything he wanted. That's not how it worked in the real world. Red lived in his world, one he created for himself. He didn't know his world was about to crumble around him. Everything was about to change. Yields would be reunited with Amber then they would get the hell out of dodge. Detective Yields called Arab. It was time to have a challenging conversation. He hoped his plan would go smoothly.

RED'S DEVIL'S

KATHY

Kathy called Big Papa when she found an older woman going by the name of Beatrice Peyton. Red's dead mother was living on the property with a teenage girl and going by the name of Willow. Kathy still could not track Naomi's whereabouts. She had a bargaining chip with Arab, so she had to work fast on finding Naomi before things got out of hand. She had to be sure Big Papa would be safe no matter what she did. He was caught up in a game of lies and deceit. Big Papa was risking his life to save Naomi. He hoped Lisa's plan would work and Arab would agree to her terms. He didn't want to let Arab anywhere near his daughter or Naomi, so he had to produce a plan of his own.

LISA

Could Lisa betray her husband, the father of her child? The child Red talked her into giving up. A man whom she spent most of her life with. They were married when Lisa was 15, and now, 15 years later, she's ready to feed him to the wolves. They may have agreed silently, but Red had gone too far. Now she was thinking of her daughter and her future. Lisa wasn't sure if Red would fit in her new tomorrow. She carefully planned it out. All she wanted was her baby girl. Her little Princess would be 15 years old by now. Lisa knew Big Papa's sister was working on it. Lisa prayed it would be good news to help lead her to her daughter. She would deal with whatever came next when she had to.

DAR

Dara was at the range every chance she got. She was becoming a perfect shot. Dara felt more than ready for Trevor. She would not hesitate after what he did to her. He needed to pay for his sins, and Dara would make sure he did. He needed to be taught how to treat a lady.

FRED

How could he help Lisa find her daughter and keep her out of harm's way? What was he going to do about Red? How can he help Arab and get him out of the way? Whatever went down, Lisa was his main priority.

TREVOR

He was not done with Dara by a long shot. He had plans for her. She wasn't going to get away with this shit. He would find her no matter where she tried to hide. He would kill her before he let her go.

RED'S DEVIL'S

JOVAN

Jovan called Britney and invited her out for dinner. He picked her up in his powder blue Ferrari and drove her to Morgantown. They went to the West Virginia football field. He rented the stadium out for the night and had his own private fireworks show for Brittany. At the same time, they ate chili dogs and pretzels. Brittany couldn't believe this was her first date. Personal fireworks show with the man she barely knew. He sure knew how to impress the ladies. This was the best date she had ever been on. She didn't want the night to end, nor did Jovon. Brittany's smile that lit up the night brighter than the fireworks. They talked all night and well into the morning. Brittany and Jovon had a connection that neither could ignore. Were her hormones going crazy, or did she really like this guy? Even though he was good friends with Red, Jovon might be a keeper.

She seemed to have caught Red fever but she was hoping she could shake it. Why wouldn't she shake that man.? What kind of spell did Red have over

RED'S DEVIL'S

Brittany that made her lust for Red insatiable? How could she resist him when she gets so turned on being around him? Maybe Jovon could change things for Brittany. Instead of wearing Red's brand, it would be nice to wear Jovon's ring instead.

    Brittany was exactly what Jovon has always wanted in a woman. She was beautiful, intelligent, honest, blunt, and upfront. There was nothing fake about Brittany. He liked the way she always said exactly what she was thinking. She was like a breath of fresh air to Jovon. Brittany made him smile while he made her blush. Jovon was glad to know she was not a stripper. Jovon thought Brittany was too intelligent to fall for Red's mind games. She was a strong, confident woman. From what he could tell, she was a no-nonsense kind of woman. It had only been a few days of spending time with her, and Jovon flew her to New York to have dinner at a rooftop restaurant. Then he took her to Miami to swim and then back to West Virginia. Every time he saw Britney, she looked stunning. Jovon couldn't keep his eyes off her. There was no way he could let Red have Brittany.

BRITTANY

Brittany was feeling a gambit of emotions from feeling very overwhelmed with all the pampering from Jovon, to her hot lust for Red, and grieving with the loss of Andrew. She knew she would never be a devil. In Red's case she lusted for him physically, but Brittany wouldn't play Red's games and didn't want to share him with the rest of the Devils. It was too much hassle for some good dick. Then there was Jovon. He was an amazing guy. He was nothing like Red or Andrew, which made him so special. Because Jovon was friends with Red Brittany wondered if he was just as ruthless as Red just better at hiding it. She didn't need two crazy psychos in her life. She was already dealing with enough shit.

It seemed like the more time she spent with Jovon, the more Red pursued her. He sent twenty dozen long-stemmed red roses. He sent her a diamond necklace and diamond bracelets. He constantly called her and would pop up at places Brittany would be by coincidence, he would say, but Brittany thought differently. He had to be following her. How else could he know where she was? Brittany was going to be sure to mention that to Jovon. It was like every time she stepped out of her front door, Red was nearby.

Brittany was getting irritated, but she was going to go to Red Devil, confront Red, and tell him to leave her alone. After that she swore she would never set foot in Red Devil ever again. She wanted to concentrate more on Jovon. When she thought about him, it made her smile. She rubbed the diamond ring she wore around her neck and thought about Andrew for a moment. She swore she would never fall for another man after losing Andrew, then Red happened, now Jovan.

She knew what she felt for Red was not love but she couldn't quite figure out exactly what it was. Jovon was almost perfect, if that's possible. Since meeting

RED'S DEVIL'S

Red and Lisa, her world has been turned upside down, but had she not met them, she would never have met Jovon. She was trying not to move so fast. Who wants to date a man that goes to strip clubs to find girlfriends? To Brittany, it seemed a little desperate. Jovon had more money than he could spend in their lifetime. The money was awesome, and the attention was great. It was not knowing just how good of friends Red and Jovan were. Were they both playing with her? Was she being set up? What was wrong with Red? Is Jovon for real, or will there be a catch? Was she ready for any of this? She returned to the night Jovon called and asked if she wanted to go swimming.

"We could go swimming since it's so hot. Do you swim?" Jovan asked Brittany.

"Yeah, I do sometimes."

"Well then pack your bags. We are flying to Miami. The best place to swim is on the beach."

"What? Right now?"

"Yes, right now. I sent a car to pick you up and bring you to the airport. I will see you when you get here." Jovan hung up the phone. Brittany was smiling from ear to ear. Who flies to the beach to go swimming!? She packed a small bag, threw on some jeans and gym shoes and put her hair in a ponytail. She figured, why to get all dolled up to swim and get your hair wet anyway.

It didn't matter to Jovon; she was the most beautiful thing he had ever seen. As soon as he saw Brittany pulling up, he began to smile. He pulled her baseball cap off and let her hair fall. He wanted to see all of the beauty that her baseball cap was hiding. He stroked her cheek, then kissed her. Then they had drinks and a blunt.

When they arrived in Miami, a car was waiting for them. They went to the beach and changed inside their cabana. When Javon saw her tits barely sitting in her bathing suit, his mouth started to water; he thought he would start drooling on himself. Brittany saw the look in Jovanna's eyes. It was like the look Red sometimes had when he looked at her.

They kissed, and Jovon undid her bathing suit top letting it fall to the floor. He laid her down and kissed her neck and her shoulders. He then began licking her breast and teasing her nipples with his wet, warm tongue. Then he squeezed her hot pussy, and she squirmed just a little. He kissed her down her stomach to her navel. He pulled her bathing suit bottoms off and spread her legs. He inserted his fingers inside and felt how ready she was. He kissed her thighs and squeezed them gently. He bit her inner thigh softly and kissed her lips and sucked her clit, spreading her legs a little wider. She wrapped her legs around his neck and arched her back, putting it right in his face. She squeezed her breasts together out of pure excitement. Whatever he was down there doing, it was perfect. Oh my God, she thought. She grabbed the back of his head, trying to push his tongue as far and deep as it could go. Her legs began to shake. She felt like she was going to pass out. Her body began convulsing and she had three orgasms back-to-back. She was sure people were on the beach. They had to hear her crying out. It was like a feeling of euphoria. This was so much different than Red. Brittany put her bathing suit back on, and they swam in the ocean.

RED'S DEVIL'S

That was the most fun she had since Andrew died. She thought she felt something on their first date at the stadium with the fireworks. But now when he kissed her, there was an electric shot shooting through her entire body. She got so wet; he turned her on like a faucet. His kiss was so intense, it felt like an explosion of the best flavors in the universe all at once. She felt passion and even love when he kissed her, intertwined his arms around her, she never wanted to let him go. Her heart beat faster when Jovon took her by the hand. He could touch her without using his hands. Brittany didn't think all this would ever be possible. She was going to tell Red that what they were doing was over. He needs to move on. Find some other girls to play with.

Brittany walked and fed Storm then got in her car and drove to Red Devil. Of course, Fred greeted her and escorted her to Red's office. Red stood up and walked from behind his desk and hugged Brittany.
"I knew you would pick me!" He squeezed her tighter.
"Pick you? What are you talking about?"

RED'S DEVIL'S

"I knew you would come back to me. I feel the same way about you. I was going crazy thinking about you being with Jovon." Red said looking at her.

"What do you know about Jovan and me?" Red said, "I know you choose me and are here exactly where you should be." He walked behind Britney and locked the door.

"What are you doing Red? I did not come for this." Red was not listening. He walked up behind Brittany and began nibbling on her ear He kissed her neck and squeezed her breast.

"Stop it, Red! I didn't come for this. Stop and listen to me." She tried to pull away.

"You know this is exactly what you came for." He started unbuttoning her shirt. Then he ripped her bra off. Britany tried to turn away. He grabbed Britany, bent her over the desk, pulled her pants down, snatched off her panties, and slid his dick deep inside her. She held on to the sides of the desk to steady herself. He was thrusting in and out, faster and faster, deeper and deeper. She moaned and pleaded but it made no difference He smacked her ass then squeezed it. He kissed and licked her from her neck down to her spine. Britney came all over him. He flipped her over, sitting her on the edge of the desk. He drove himself back inside her with low, slow strokes while they kissed. She wrapped her arms around his neck and her legs around his waist. Then he picked her up and started fucking the shit out of her. They both came together. As soon as Red put her down, she slapped him and started getting dressed.

"What the hell was that for, Bold Britney?" Red rubbed his face.

"I told you I didn't come for this! Could you leave me alone!? Stop showing up everywhere I go! Stop sending flowers and jewelry! Stop calling me and follow me! I said I couldn't be a devil and I don't share. You have to face it. You can't have everything you want! Goodbye, Red. Don't call again." She slammed the diamond bracelet and necklace on Red's desk and left the office.

"I take what I want!" He yelled through the closed door.

RED'S DEVIL'S

Brittany was furious with herself. It felt so good but now she felt so bad. It's not like she and Jovon were in a committed relationship. So why did she feel guilty all of a sudden? What the hell was that about Red!? How did she just let that happen? Did she try her best to resist? There was Red. And she got exactly what she came there for. Brittany prayed that Red would get the picture and leave her alone. If that was really what she wanted. Brittany was trying to get together and realized she had left something in his office. It wasn't worth going. She could always go to Victoria's Secret and get a new bra. She couldn't trust herself around Red. It was best that she kept her distance from Red from now on.

AMBER

Amber didn't know how many days she had been in the toy box. There were no windows, and the walls were black and red. There was no clock on the wall to tell the time or what day it was. Red brought her food three times a day and kept her locked in. There was a bathroom and a shower for her. He even bought clothes and shoes for her. He did not touch or try to force himself on her. Amber was trying to figure out precisely what he had planned for her. Someone would be looking for her. She had family and clients. Someone was going to notice her being gone.

She thought Yields must be dead, or he was in on it all along, helping Red to claim her as his prize? Did she make a fool out of herself by falling for Yields? That was not part of her plan. She planned to pretend to fall for him to get information about Red that she could use to get him off her back. Then she found herself falling for Yields. Even after finding out, he was a police officer. She hadn't even used that to her advantage. Now she had no idea if he was dead or alive. She didn't know how she could escape this self-made prison. Red had her in. She knew one thing for sure. If and when she got out, Red would pay for this. She would be sure of it.

Amber had to produce a plan to save her life by convincing Red that she would be a devil. "You finally decided to become a devil?" Red asked Amber.

"Yes, I will be a devil. I'm serious this time. I will come to work for you. No strings attached."

"You agreed to fill out the paperwork and follow the rules? Oh, and of course, get your tattoo?" Amber swallowed hard.

"Yes, Red. I will." He had a big grin on his face.

"In that case, welcome home, Ambitious Amber. Welcome to the Red Devil!" Amber tried to smile; It just wasn't working out very well.

"Fred will surely get you to your car and safely home. I will see you tonight."

Red led her to the door, and Fred escorted her out.

Amber got in her car and sped out of the parking lot. She was trying to decide if she was going to go to the police or if she should try to find detective Yields. Maybe his plan didn't sound too bad after all. There had to be something she could do. Amber decided to tell Yields that she knew he was a police officer, and that Red was interfering with her life and her business. He had to be stopped. She was treating these women like property instead of people. Now he wanted to own Amber. She saw that Red would stop at nothing to add her to his collection. Yields was going to have to be her ticket out of this mess.

YIELDS

Yields didn't tell Amber he was a cop because he had been suspended indefinitely because he could not pass his psych evaluation. He may not even be a police officer anymore. All he could think about was Amber and if she was safe, and how he could help her. What was he willing to do for love? Yields was wrecking his brain when his phone rang.

" Yields, this is Amber." She was whispering." Come to my house."

"Oh, my God! I'm so glad you are ok. I'm on my way., get your gun, and don't open the door for anyone."

Amber locked her windows and doors and waited for Yields to get there. Yields was speeding and trying to get to Amber as fast as he could. He didn't want to take the chance of losing her again. He would come for her and take her away from all the danger.

ARAB

Arab, Fred, Lisa, and Big Papa were in the dining area of the Red Devils. They gave him some of the information Kathy had discovered. The two properties were under Red's mother's name. But no sign of Naomi. The girl living on the property was much too young to be Naomi. Arab told him. He will be in touch once he has more information to give them. He had a little legwork to do he was. He was a hands-on guy; he didn't need anyone to handle his business. He planned on finding Naomi and bringing her home and if anyone tried to stand in his way, they would be removed permanently. Once he had more to go on, he would confront Red with what he found, then he would decide what to do about it.   Arab considered visiting a dear friend until he heard Red may have something to do with Naomi disappearance.

RED'S DEVIL'S

He had to book a flight from Paris, France, to Dijon. He needed to see where this trail led him. He prayed he was one step closer to being with Naomi again. The thought alone put a smile on his face. It had been way too long. He didn't care what he had to do to get her back; things would return as they should. Then he would deal with everything else. Fred quickly called Arab and told him about Naomi and how he would help him find her. That was one thing Red never shared with him the whereabouts of Naomi. Fred told him everything about Red and Amber. The faster he finds Naomi; the faster Arab can leave West Virginia. Arab booked his flight to Paris, France. He rented a car and drove to the address in Dijion. He took pictures of the house and then waited to see if anyone would come in or leave out. He had nothing but time on his hands.

AMBER

She was so happy to see Yields, and he held her tight and let her cry. She was angry and frustrated.

RED'S DEVIL'S

She refused to allow Red to come in and screw up her life. She wanted the bullshit to be over and done with. She needed a way out.

"I'm so sorry I wasn't there." He rubbed her hair.

"I want this to be over." She felt like she could kill Red with her bare hands.

"Just a few more days, and this will be all over long as you play your part."

He kissed Amber and pulled her onto his lap. He had been so worried about her. He thought he had lost her and never wanted to feel that way again. Amber was happy they didn't kill Yields. She had been just as worried about him as he was about her. They both knew they had to do something fast. Amber would only have to tolerate Red for a bit longer, soon everything would fall into place. Time for Amber to go to work on her first night as a devil. Would she be able to play it off and be convincing? She was about to find out.

When she arrived at the Red Devil, Fred walked her to Red's office. Amber hesitated to step inside. She was frozen with fear, scared that she would be held against her will again. When Fred left the office, Amber pulled her gun out and pointed at a Red. "If you ever try some shit like that again- snatching me and holding me captive, I will blow your fucking head off!" She then left his office and entered the dressing room to prepare for her first set. She wanted this night to be over. She wanted her life back and knew how to get it back, even if it meant she had to die.

ARAB

Arab watched an older white lady and a young—preteen-looking girl go inside and turn the lights on. Arab waited a few minutes before he walked to the door and knocked on it. The woman answered the door and invited him in. He told her he was a friend of Reds, and that he was sent to make sure she and the girl were ok. The woman wasn't so sure about his story. Red never told her that he would send someone if he couldn't make it. He said he did not have contact with them for months before they packed up and left the country. Finally, after getting the older woman comfortable with him and after so many drinks, he had all the information he needed. That sneaky ass mutherfucker was off the hook. Arab would keep his findings to himself for now, until he returned to West Virginia with his surprising news. He was very eager to see how eager Lisa was going to save her so-called family.

LISA

Arab called Lisa and told her to meet him at the Cracker Barrel in Clarksburg, he had something important to show her. Lisa was damn near running stop signs and red lights to get to Clarksburg. She found Arab sitting in the booth alone. Lisa joined him.

"So, what do you have for me Arab?" Lisa was very anxious.

"Take a look at these." He slid his phone to her and watched her scroll through the pictures. There were several pictures of an older lady and a teenage girl. Then he wrote two names on a sheet of paper and slid it to Lisa.

"The girl is 15." Arab got up and left the restaurant, leaving Lisa there in disbelief. It was Red's mother and their daughter.

RED

Red received a frantic phone call from his mother, crying and apologizing for telling their business to a stranger. She was crying and begging for forgiveness. While he was trying to calm his mother down, Lisa walked into his office and grabbed the phone from Red and hung it up. "You lying, selfish son of a bitch! 15 years Red! 15 years!" Red looked at the pictures on Lisa's phone that she had just gotten from Arab. "Listen., Let me just explain."

"Explain. I should kill your ass right now! You asshole. My daughter...you've had our daughter all this time, and you kept her away from me! I'm going

to kill you!" Lisa charged at Red, but Fred came in and grabbed Lisa. He was trying to hold her back.
" Let me go.! You are no better than Red. Fifteen years of hurt, sadness, pain, and worry. You let me suffer for 15 years. Why couldn't you not tell me? Don't ever touch me again. You two deserve each other and everything that's coming to you."

Lisa stormed out of the office and left the club. She was furious. She hoped he got precisely what was coming to him. It was over between her and Red. There was nothing left for her at the Red Devils, nothing and no one. All Red could do was sit there and stare into space. How was he going to clean this mess up? He knew Lisa would never forgive him, and he would never forgive himself. Now he had Arab to worry about, Naomi, and Big Papa. How could he keep Naomi safe? He would have to move her soon before it was too late.

FRED

Fred knew this would happen eventually. If only he could get Lisa to understand and hear him out. He was only trying to protect her to the best of his ability. He knew he should have told Lisa a long time ago, now it was too late. She would hate him for the rest of her life, and he couldn't blame her at all. Fred knew what he was risking when he decided to keep the secret. The only thing he could do was try and make things right if possible. There were a few loose ends he had to manage, then he could try to mend his relationship with Lisa. He knew she would not be around too much longer. He knew Lisa would run to Paris and get her only child. There was no stopping her. He may have to take some drastic measures. He didn't care what happened to him anymore as long as Lisa and her daughter were safe. He was ready to face the music. To pay for his sin and to be rid of all these terrible burdens he was carrying around. He made a phone call and then started preparing for the consequences.

NAOMI

RED'S DEVIL'S

Naomi was 22 years old, 5 feet,2 inches with dark brown eyes. The dark brown complexion and built like a shapely brick house. She was Arab's adopted sister. Arab fell in love with her when his parents bought her home. He did not look at her as a sister. They did not share the same blood. He became her legal guardian once his parents died in an unfortunate car accident. Hit head-on by a drunk driver.

Naomi became his property. She belonged solely to him. He started having sex with her when she turned 15 years old. He controlled her every movement and kept a close eye on her. He would always find her every time she managed to sneak off, that was until she went to Red's. Once Red found out who she was, he helped her get away from Arab and his controlling and abusive behavior. She begged him to help her to get away. She didn't tell Big Papa because she didn't want him hurt. She never even told him she was pregnant but to be fair she didn't know until she was on the run and had Red help her. Red talked her into giving up her child for their safety then he moved her to Amsterdam, where no one could think of looking for her there. Of course, she changed her name and had fake IDs and passports. Naomi lived in Amsterdam for five years, being away from her daughter and not knowing where she left her or who with.

Naomi didn't have a choice. She did not want her daughter anywhere near Arab? She knew he would use her daughter as a bargaining chip to tighten his grip on her. Naomi prayed everyday that Big Papa and her daughter were healthy, happy, and safe. She knew just how crazy Arab was, that's why she agreed to leave Big Papa and their daughter. Big Papa and Naomi didn't realize how close Arab was to finding out everything. Naomi could not allow that to happen. She would die first or kill Arab herself. She refused to return to that private hell she lived in with Arab. He tormented her daily for years. She would never go back to that. Naomi had to move fast. She had a new life that she was going to protect...period!

RED'S DEVIL'S

JOVON

Jovan couldn't wait to see Brittany again. He planned on flying her to Vegas to show her a good time. He couldn't possibly share her with anyone. He fantasized about all the things he was going to do to her. He wanted to skip dinner and eat her for dessert. He called his dream girl, then went to pick her up.
"What are you in the mood for tonight?" He looked at Brittany; She was looking mouthwatering. He was getting hard just looking at her.
"Whatever you want to do is fine with me." Brittany did a little spin for Jovon. She had on a sleek black gown with some silver stilettos. A necklace around her neck with a diamond heart ring and a pair of silver earrings. She smelled delicious. He wanted her right there and then. "Walk in front of me. So, I can see your ass." She did her catwalk for him.
"Tonight is all about you." Jovon told Brittany.
"You look like you want to do dirty things to me." Brittany said to Jovon.
"You have no idea how badly I want you right now. I can't believe I met you."

RED'S DEVIL'S

"I wore this dress just for you. I can't wait to show you what's under it." Britney laughed.

"That's not funny; you're teasing me with all your sexiness." He pulled Brittany close to him. She smelled like Jimmy Choo, and she looked finger-licking good.

"I'll tell you a secret; you're what's missing from between my legs." He kissed her neck and said "I like licking you." They both smiled.

"We should go if you keep looking at me like that. We will not have to go somewhere a little more private.

"I can't stop thinking about what you did to me the last time we were together." She kissed Jovon and grabbed his dick, giving a light squeeze.

"I'm always in the mood for you. "

They headed to the airport for their flight to Las Vegas; Brittany had never been to Vegas before. She was overly excited about the trip and about being with Jovan. They boarded his private jet and were off to Las Vegas. Red wasn't on either of their minds. He

RED'S DEVIL'S

took Brittany to Hell's Kitchen for an exquisite meal from the greatest chef in the world.

"You're terrible at pretending you don't want me." Brittany said to Jovon.

"I'm thinking about how amazing your body is right now. He sipped on his glass of red wine." I will tell you a little secret; I'm dripping wet and ready to explode." She drank some of her wine and looked at Jovon. He was looking at her with so much admiration on his face. They enjoyed their dinner, went to The MGM Casino, and did some gambling. Brittany gambled every once in a while, just never in Vegas. She was having a perfect time. He wined and dined her and showed her a great time; then they flew back to West Virginia.

On the flight home, things heated up.

"First. You're going to take of your cloths then I'm going to suck and fuck you."

"Is that an order?" He playfully asked Brittany.

"Take your clothes off, lie down, and shut up."

"Ok, pleasing you is my only purpose." Jovon followed Brittany's orders and did just as he was told.

RED'S DEVIL'S

Brittany lay between his legs and started sucking his dick, giving him long, slow slurps up and down his dick. Her mouth was so wet. She had a mean head game. She sucked and licked and caressed his nuts. Then she climbed on top of him and started riding him backward while she squeezed his nuts. He kissed and squeezed her ass cheeks and watched that pink wet pussy go up and down on his dick. The pilot came across the intercom saying they were about to land.

" Better cum with me so we can land this baby." Jovan told Brittany right before he was about to bust. Brittany jumped off his dick and sat on his face while she sucked his dick. She came all down his throat and all over his face just he burst in her mouth.
"You just painted my face. With your juices." Jovan licked his lips and smiled and said.
"Dessert was delicious."

A car was waiting for them at the airport. Jovan drove Brittany home. He walked her to the door, gave her a good night kiss, and watched her safely into her house. As she closed the door and he turned away, gunshots rang in the air and the sound of a car speeding off. Brittany ran to the door and opened it to find Jovon lying on the ground bleeding. Brittany screamed and ran into the house to call 911. She silently prayed for Jovon to be ok. Who the hell did this, and why? What the fuck was going on? Why would someone want to hurt Jovon? Brittany and Storm stayed by Jovon's side until the police and ambulance arrived.

TREVOR

Trevor parked across the street from the Red Devil and watched Dara pull up. As soon as Fred walked her inside, Trevor ran to the parking lot and hid behind the garage until the camera turned out of his view. He ran to Dara's car, broke in and hid on the back floor. He had had enough; it was time to teach Dara a lesson. He wasn't giving her up that easily. He was going to take what was his. Hours passed, and the club was finally closing. All the dancers were being escorted to their cars and leaving. Dara climbed into her car and drove home. Red had one of his security team follow her home. They watched her go inside, then drove off. She felt more relaxed knowing she was being guarded. She had a long night and made lots of money. She was ready for a shower and a glass of wine, then off to bed she would go.

Dara turned on the shower and got undressed. She thought she heard a sound. She wrapped her towel around her and checked where the noise came from. She entered her bedroom and sat on the edge of the bed, when Trevor walked into the bedroom
"Hello my love, I see you are waiting for Daddy to come home and fuck you good the way only I can." He smiled at Dara and thought he was about to take her right there and have his way with her.
"Yes, Trevor, I've been waiting for you. You see, I knew you were in the back of my car. Your Obsession cologne gave you away. I've been waiting for you to get what you deserve."
"That's what I like to hear."

RED'S DEVIL'S

Trevor walked towards Dara, and she pulled the 9-millimeter from under her pillow. She then fired and emptied her clip in him just like Lisa said. Trevor was not going to be hurting her anymore. She got dressed and called 911. Then she called the Red Devil and told Lisa what had just occurred. Dara took her power back. She no longer felt violated and helpless, and she didn't have to be scared anymore. Now Trevor was getting raped in hell! Never to hurt her again.

LISA

Lisa got her passport out of her safe, packed her bag, and reserved her flight to Paris, France. She was finally on her way to meet her mother-in-law and daughter, Willow, who was now 15 years old. All this time, Red built a relationship with their daughter. He kept it a secret from Lisa, robbing her of her daughter's life. They could have been a real family. She could have been a mother to her child and a wife to Red, only Red had other plans. Lisa was on her way to finally meet her daughter after all these years. She couldn't believe she would be with her daughter

RED'S DEVIL'S

in a matter of hours. Lisa was going to take her daughter and never look back. The Red Devil was history, and her future was with her daughter. There was no place for Red.

FRED

Fred was walking one of the dancers to the car when he was ambushed. A masked man knocked him out cold and dragged him behind the trash can. The masked man pulled off his mask and walked into the Red Devil. Then he walked into Red's office unannounced.

ARAB

Arab had someone in Paris watching Kathy's house. She was in the process of moving to her new place with Big Papa and Naomi's baby. His henchman called Arab every hour, giving him details and sending pictures. Arab wasn't ready to make his move just yet. He had some unfinished business with Red.

KATHY

Kathy noticed a strange man outside. He had been watching her the whole time. She was moving her stuff into the new place. She was scared and called Red to see if it was one of his men.

DARA

After being questioned by the police, her adrenaline finally went down, and the severity of the situation hit her. She had the urge to go shopping, it always helped when she had a stressful situation. She just killed someone. She killed someone she wanted. She remembered feeling as if she could not live without the man she used to love more than herself, or so it seemed at times. Trevor was dead. He could never hurt her again and Dara was a killer. At that moment, she knew she had to do it, and she did it. She wasn't sure if she wanted him dead, she would have been okay with him going to jail. Then she would have to worry about him stalking and harassing her. Now he was gone for good. No more Trevor and no more fears. She needed to see Red.

YIELDS

He dropped the mask on the desk and pulled out his gun.

"So finally, you grew a pair?" Red asked Yields.

"I have finally stopped being used and played like a fool by you!"

"That's why you have a gun pointed in my face?" Red stays very still. He didn't want to make any sudden moves to startle Yields.

"Tell me, best friend, what is this about? Did Arab offer you money? Don't tell me you're here because of Amber; let me guess... you think you're in love. You do this at least once or twice a year. You think you have found your soulmate, then you get bored and move on. You're not in love with Amber. Learn to control your hormones. There are plenty of women here at the Red Devil. You can choose whomever you like."

"Thank you, Red but I love Amber; We belong together and want to be together. I'm tired of your sloppy seconds. I love Amber, and we are going to be together! Now either you agree to let us be and leave us alone or I'm going to kill you. We are going to leave town; you won't ever see us again. I need your word. I will walk out of here and never look back; if not, I'm sorry to say I can't leave you here to track us down. I don't want to live always looking over my shoulder. It shouldn't have to be like this. You have any and everything you could want. Why can't I have this one? When is it going to be my turn?" Yields was still pointing the gun at Red.

"Put the gun down, Yields. You know what would happen here. I mean, look around you. There's nowhere for you to go. Think…. Do you want to die here tonight, at this very moment, and risk losing the woman of your dreams? Then it will be all for nothing. Amber would still be mine. You see, it doesn't matter if you're dead or alive. Amber is mine."

Yields was about to pull the trigger and take his chances until Dara walked in unexpectedly, Yields lowered his gun, hoping she didn't see it.

"Daring Dara, how are you feeling? Do you need some time off, or were you here to play?" Red pulled Dara close to him and stroked her hair.

"We will talk soon, Red. Real soon. Yields walked out of Red's office and left the building.

DARA

Dara sat on the edge of Red's desk smiling." What was that all about? Isn't he your best friend?" She pointed towards the door.

"He was having women problems. I was giving him some advice. He didn't take it too well. His ego is bruised. Don't worry about him; how do you feel about Trevor?"

RED'S DEVIL'S

Dara shrugged her shoulders." I don't know yet; my brain has not processed everything yet. I don't know how I'm supposed to feel right now. I feel numb and miss feeling your hands all over me."

Dara bit her bottom lip." I can't get enough of your body."

Just as Red leaned over to kiss Dara, Arab barged into Red's office. This triggered Daras reflexes. She pulled her gun out and pointed it at the door. For a moment, she forgot Trevor was dead by her own hands. Dara snapped back to reality and lowered the gun. Red looked at her, admiring her fast reflex. He saw she could manage herself; he was lucky she was on his side.

"Calm down, darling. This is a friend of mine. Arab, come in and have a seat. Can you excuse us, Daring Dara.? I need a moment to catch up with my dear old friend." Red picked a bottle of Hennessy and two shot glasses.

"I see you need your privacy, so it would not be nice of me to blow you right now?" She blew a dark blue bubble with her gum, popped it, and left the office.

RED'S DEVIL'S

As she was heading out the exit, she saw the security guard, Fred talking to three other men in the parking lot. She could tell they were having a heated discussion, but she could not hear them. When Fred noticed her, they all stopped talking. Fred walked her to her car; he searched inside of it before she got in.

Dara pulled out of the lot, still trying to process what had happened. She almost shot Red's friend. Trevor was gone. So why does she feel so afraid? Maybe it wasn't a good idea for her to carry a gun. She might hurt someone that she didn't mean to. On the other hand, Trevor was dead, so she could lock the gun up and never use it again. Maybe she could take a self-defense class, but she thought that kind of stuff only worked on TV. She needed a drink, so she went to EBO's and had a couple of shots of Hennessy. She needed to clear her head. What she needed was some good head and a good pounding. Sex was her #1 stress reliever. It seemed as if shooting came in at a close 2nd. She needed Red right now. Maybe she should drive back to the Red Devil. He always stayed late; some nights, he wouldn't even leave the club. Dara needed to cum. She needed to release, relax, and relate. Right now, the only one that could help her was Red. Red's friend would have to excuse her. They can catch up later. Dara needed to cum now. Dara decided to shower and change. Once dressed, she hopped in her car and drove back to the Red Devil.

ARAB

"A dear old friend? Is that what we are Red? I see you still have a wide palette when it comes to women. Tigers never change their stripes or so I'm told."

Arab took his shot of Hennessy, then poured another. The whole time he was looking directly at Red.

"I know we used to be remarkably close friends, then you stopped coming around. I know you are here for a reason, and it's not to talk about my women." Arab poured another shot and drank it.

"We must have different meanings for the word friend. When a friend gives a friend a rule, the friend should respect the relationship and not break that rule. A real friend doesn't lie to his friend for five years!"

Red stood up and said to Arab, "I did not just go against you. It wasn't like that. When she came here, she used a different name. She looked different from the pictures you showed me. I hadn't seen her since she was a young kid. As soon as I found out who she was, I told her she had to go. By then, it was too late." Red took another shot.

"Too late for what?" Arab was gritting his teeth.

"She had fallen in love. I told her to go back home to you. She was afraid and asked me to put her up for a while. She told me she would call you and have you come and pick her up. I put her on a plane and hadn't seen or heard from her in five years. You never came looking, so I just assumed she went home." Red sat back down behind his desk.

"Why didn't you call when you discovered her true identity?"

"She was young and afraid. She said she wanted to give you a few days to settle down before she went back home. You never reached out." Red was watching Arab, and his security monitors all simultaneously, trying to anticipate Arabs' next move. "I did some digging out on my own. I even took a little trip to a place you are familiar with. Paris is lovely this time of year." Red almost choked on his Hennessy.

"Lovely house, lovely people living in lovely houses are living ugly lies. Just like you, my old, dear friend. You lied to me. You knew where Naomi was, and you knew she was pregnant. You know the father, and you helped her hide the baby and helped her disappear! You helped her run away from me! YOU HELPED HER RUN AWAY FROM ME!

Arab stood up and threw the chair across the room. Fred charged into the room to see both men standing up, facing one another, looking like they would rip each other apart.

"Everything in here ok, Red?" Fred asked, glancing over the room, trying to assess the situation. He didn't see any weapons. He figured they would be out by now if either one of them were armed. Fred knew

RED'S DEVIL'S

from experience Red, nor Arab would ever get their own hands dirty. They have people for that.

"Everything is simply fine, Fred; you can leave. Go back to your post." Fred left and closed the door.

"Listen, leave Big Papa out of this. He didn't know who she was either. He never knew about the baby. He's innocent, and he treated her very well. He was exceptionally good to her for the short time they were together. Naomi was afraid you might try to make her give up the baby or use the baby to keep her home with you. I didn't want to involve Big Papa but wanted the baby to be with family, that would assure me the baby would be well taken care of." Red took another shot. The bottle was half empty.

"Let me get this straight. You hired her, and she started fucking your cook? She got pregnant then. You sent her off to some secret hideout and kept it away from me for five years? While supporting the woman that is claiming my niece as her child? I'm supposed to believe you didn't know who she was and that you thought she would come back to me in a few days. You sent her out of town secretly to give me a chance to calm down?!MUTHERFUCKER!" Arab was infuriated. He wanted to strangle the lives right out of Red.

"I will tell you everything. What else do you need to know?' Red opened another bottle of Hennessy.

"You will still be breathing tomorrow because you made sure my baby niece was safe and cared for, because of that, you live. Now that your number one devil or wife knows about mommie dearest and long-lost daughter Willow, she will probably take you out herself." Arab smiled at the thought.

"You already tried to have me killed at the airport when I came back from Paris." Arab looked at Red, and he was confused.

"I never tried to have you killed. If I wanted you dead, I would only have to do it once. You would be dead and cold on a slab. I'm going to give you an option, or rather a choice. Choose the right one...all can be forgiven. Choose the wrong one...it won't be a good ending for you. If you send Naomi home and I get my niece, your family will be safe from harm. Big Papa is never to have any contact ever again. I will raise the child as mine. He stays away, but he lives. If not, you already know the answer, or maybe you want me to raise Willow as my own as well. She looks a lot like her mommy, Lisa. I see good looks run the family. So, what will it be, dear old friend?"

AMBER

Amber got a call from one of her clients on the police force; he told her to check her e-mail. He found something about detective Yields. Amber opened the e-mail, and she couldn't believe what she was reading. He had been suspended because he was a suspect in the case of two West Virginia missing women, both were last seen with him at the time of their disappearance. They didn't have enough evidence to charge him. Both of the women had files with complaints against him, saying he was stalking them and claimed that they were his soul mate. He was ordered to go to therapy but did not comply. He was under investigation right now. The two women

RED'S DEVIL'S

were never found. One girl had been missing for three years, and the other for over a year and a half. They said he got angry whenever the woman would not leave their jobs and run off with him.

She couldn't believe it. Yields was on psych meds, and it was obvious that he wasn't taking them because now he is completely obsessed with Amber. She fell right into his trap. Now she had two psychos to be afraid of. How the hell did she get caught up in this bullshit? Amber was catching feelings for Yields. First, he never told Amber that he was a police officer, now she finds out all this shit! How could she have been so stupid and blind? He seemed so normal. She thought he had an innocent crush or something, not that he was some psycho killer. He seemed normal. She thought he just had passion and harmless desire, not some psycho killer. Her life was in danger the whole time she was with him. Anything could set him off at any moment.

RED'S DEVIL'S

BIG PAPA

Big Papa heard the whole conversation between Red and Arab, so did Fred. Fred had bugged Red's office without him knowing it. Big Papa had to warn his sister and ensure his daughter was safe. They still didn't know where Naomi was and didn't think Red would tell them. Big Poppa would never agree to stay out of his daughter's life. He had already missed the first five years and planned to be around for a long time. He also wanted the mother of his child to come home safe and unharmed. Even though Red was trying to save Big Papas life, he was using Naomi and their daughter as a bargaining chip to do it. That did not sit well with Big Papa at all. He had to find Naomi before Arab, or he might never see her again; she may even end up dead.

YIELDS

He should have just killed Red while he had the chance. If that bitch Dara hadn't walked in and interrupted them the deed would have been done. Maybe he should have killed her too. Nobody would miss a stripper. His head was hurting and the voices were getting loud again. Where were his damn pills? He forgot to refill his prescription. Yields hadn't needed them anyway. He was feeling simply fine. He just needed a clear head when he was around his one true love, Amber. She loved him, and he loved her. They were meant to be. He knew that from the moment he saw her. Nothing and no one will keep them apart. Amber wasn't like the last two girls. She was different; she understood him. She cared about him, and she trusted him. She was going to be his wife. She was unafraid to leave her past behind and start a new life with him.

Fuck Red! He doesn't know how much in love he and Amber were. Red was just jealous. He was mad because Amber chose him and not Red. Amber belonged to him. Red was wrong. He didn't know what the hell he was talking about. Yields was going to marry Amber; he wouldn't have to hurt her like the other girls. They didn't love him. Not like Amber loved him. He's not a stalker. He just wants to be around the woman he loves as much as possible. He wanted to shower her with love and gifts. He wanted to spend every moment with her. He would prove his love to her daily for the rest of his life. If Red would not agree to let him keep Amber; then, he would just have to kill Red. He should have already killed him. He was a detective. He could kill and get away with it or frame somebody else for the murder. No one would be the wiser. That's probably why those two women's bodies haven't been found, they never would be. He had to get to Amber before Red did. It was time to see just how much Amber loved him.

REECE

During all the drama, all the sex, all the lies and secrets, one devil went out of her way not to be noticed, but she always seemed to be around. Always listening, Always watching. Her name was Reece. She had been a devil for over a year or a little longer.

RED'S DEVIL'S

Reece was a beautiful chocolate girl. She was from Detroit, but she moved to West Virginia a few years ago for a change of scenery. She wanted something different in her life other than working for minimum wage. That's when Red found her and made her a devil. She was 5-foot-7 inches, 150 pounds, double D titties, and a fat ass. Reece had pretty brown eyes and a beautiful smile. She did a little stripping in Detroit while living with her mother and older sister.

Reece to move to West Virginia when she and the guy she was engaged to broke up, then he passed away. She was running from the pain and was looking for a fresh start in a new place. Reece was doing some shopping in Morgantown when her truck broke down. She was standing on the side of her truck with the hood open. The truck was smoking so badly that it looked like it was on fire. When Red saw her, he knew he had to have her. Red introduced himself and gave her one of his business cards. He offered to help Reece. She didn't know anything about cars so she just was more than happy for his assistance.

RED'S DEVIL'S

"I'm Red. I own and run The Red Devil. You should come and audition; you would fit in well with all my beautiful devils. I operate a very classy place. Have you ever danced before?" Red reached out his hand out, and Reece shook his hand.

"I'm Reece; I'm not from around here; I just relocated from Detroit, MI. Could you lead me to a good mechanic? A mechanic that won't try to overcharge me because I am a woman?"

"I can call my guy and have him take you to the shop. He will fix you right up. Work for me; you will drive your dream car in a month, I guarantee you. What is your dream car Reece?"

"A red drop-top Mercedes is my dream car."

"Come work at Red Devil, and if you don't make enough to buy your dream car, I will buy it for you, scouts honor. Red crosses his heart with his finger.

"What? Wait, you will buy me a drop-top Mercedes if I come to collaborate with you? If I become a devil? Is this some joke?"

"I don't play when it comes to business. How about I get your car towed and have a car drive you home, then pick you up when you are ready? When you're ready to come to the club, check my place out, and see how you like it, I will have them drop it off when your car is repaired. At the club, you can come to drive yourself home whenever you are ready to leave. How does that sound?"

Reese bit her bottom lip, trying to decide if she should trust this strange white guy that looked like he belonged on a GQ billboard. He could be a serial killer. She saw many crazy stories about West Virginia on the ID channel. She decided to accept the offer. Plus, it might be fun. Reece loved to party and go to strip clubs. Maybe she can make a couple of dollars to get her truck fixed. Red said, she should have her dream car in a month. That would be incredible! That's a hell of a lot of money. Red had to be exaggerating. Strippers don't make that kind of money, but right now, any money was better than no money, and Reece didn't have any money. It's not like she had anything to lose.

Red's car dropped her off at home so she could shower and change. Then she had to find something to wear. Red said his place was classy, so she wanted to dress accordingly. She found a sexy form-fitting red strapless gown with red bottom heels and some costume jewelry for her accessories. Reece did her hair and makeup and called the driver's number. Reece told the driver that she was ready to be picked up. The car pulled up in 10 minutes, and Reece was on her way to the Red Devil as one of Red's special guests. When Reece arrived, she could not believe her eyes. Red did not exaggerate. The Red Devil was a very classy place. She had never seen anything like it. The club she danced at in Detroit was like a hole in the wall compared to Red Devils. All the dancers looked like models. They were all so beautiful. Red told her she would fit right in with his devils. Reece saw all the money the dancers were making and was incredibly surprised. She had never seen a stripper get tipped like that. Reece started thinking she might take the offer that Red gave her. She started to picture herself in her fire engine red drop-top Mercedes. What if she saved enough to move to the Caribbean like she always dreamed? Then she would visit Spain

RED'S DEVIL'S

for the summer. After Red gave her the tour, he took Reece into his office so she could fill out the necessary paperwork. That's when he told her about the devil horn tattoo. Reece already had three tattoos; one more wouldn't hurt, especially if it would lead to driving a new Mercedes.

"I think I'm going to enjoy working here." Red slid her the list of rules. Reece read them over. Some of the rules made him seem controlling; she signed them anyway. All she could think of was a new car in the Caribbean.

Reece stayed and worked her month, and on that last day of the month, just as Red had promised her, she had her fire engine red drop-top Mercedes. Reece had been there ever since. When Reece first came to the Red Devil, Lisa didn't trust her. Lisa always thought there was something Reece was hiding or that she was not being candid about. There was just something about Reece that rubbed Lisa the wrong way. Red thought it was just Lisa being jealous or overprotective. Red always wrote Lisa off when she brought it up. Reece was always in the shadows, walking in on private conversations or being out of place. Hanging around all the time and always asking questions. She was just too nosey for her own good. She was a good devil, followed the rules, and brought in many high-paying customers and current go-getters. She was making good money by making many fantasies come true. If it was role play, threesomes, or S&M, she was down for it. One thing she was good at was pleasing men or a woman. Reece even had a few women customers who were her regulars. Lisa felt Reece was up to no good. She never felt comfortable around Reece. She always kept her distance from her. It seemed like Reece was always watching Lisa from across the room.

LISA

Lisa was on the plane to Paris to find her daughter. She had no clue what Arab would do to Red and Big Papa. But that wasn't her problem anymore. Her only concern was Willow. All this time, Red had their daughter hidden from her. Why would he do that to her and to their daughter? How can you keep a mother away from her child all that time? Were so many years stolen from her by her husband? She would do anything for Red, this was the ultimate betrayal. She could never forgive him. Things would never be the same again. Lisa left the Red Devil for good; she would get the only family she had left.

BRITTANY

Brittany was at the hospital with Jovon. The bullet went through his left shoulder and didn't hit any major arteries. He would be in pain but live. Brittany was so glad he was ok. She wanted to know who was behind this; why would someone want to hurt Jovon? The only person she could think of was Red. Did he go as far as to try to kill Jovon so he could have Britney for himself? Would he go that far? Did she have to worry about her safety? Was her life in danger as well? What was she going to do about it?

RED'S DEVIL'S

Brittany needed answers; she knew she would only get them from Red himself.

REECE

Reece knew that some severe shit was going down in the Red Devil. She had to figure out precisely what it was. This could blow her story out of the water. She needed more details and many photos, which she had plenty of. All she had to do was put the puzzle together. Once she had all the pieces.

FRED

"I told you to make it look real., you knocked me out cold. That was not the plan!"

"I had to make it look convincing, just in case." Fred was rubbing his head where Yields left a knot on it.

"You didn't even take care of him as we planned! He is still alive!"

RED'S DEVIL'S

"I couldn't; that Dara chick walked into the office." Fred did not want to hear the excuses. Yields were supposed to take Red out, and all their problems would be solved. If only they could find Naomi. How would they get that out of Red? Fred had to figure out how to help Big Papa and Naomi with their baby. Fred thought he would never see his baby girl Lisa again. If he did, she would not have anything to do with him. All because he chose to keep Red's secrets, now Fred is paying for it in the worst way.

BRITTANY

All this nonsense with Red, and the Red Devil was too much for Brittany. She had gotten into Red's web of lies and secrets. Now she was being used as a pawn in Red's mind game. That man had serious issues. Now, Jovon was hurt because of it. It was the only explanation. Why else would Jovon have been shot if it were not because of Red? Why couldn't he accept that Brittany would not be joining his family, becoming a devil? It was time to put a stop to Red and his sick games. Brittany felt so sorry for Jovon getting mixed up in all of this. She never expected Red to go as far as trying to have someone killed, all because he wanted to be with her. Who does crazy shit like that? Did he think he could force Brittany to be a devil? To just run her life and have her be loyal. Hell no! It was not going to happen. Brittany was beginning to fear Red and what he might do to her or what he may have planned for her.

KATHY

Kathy packed a small bag for her and Big Papa's daughter. She snuck out of the back door of the house. She ran a few blocks and waved a taxi down. Then she checked herself into the nearest hotel she could find; then the car drove up to see what she needed to do next. Kathy couldn't live on the run with a 5-year-old girl. They would not have any everyday life. She had to contact her brother and let him know she was safe.

JOVON

Jovon was in a lot of pain. He could not drive, so he had a car come to pick them up. They went to one of his many homes. That Jovon had in Morgantown. He needed a hot shower and some strong pain pills. He could not understand who would want to try and kill him. Luckily, they were not a particularly good shot. The masked gunman shot at Jovon at least six times, but he was only hit once. After Brittany told him everything about Red and Red Devils, everything seemed more precise now. Something had to be done about Red. He took things way too far. Someone needed to stop him before anyone else got hurt. Or worse, they may end up dead." Leave your job and come with me, where we can make love daily." Jovon said to Brittany." Wow, are you serious? You want me to drop everything and fly off with you to

RED'S DEVIL'S

Africa?" Brittany was caught off guard by his question. "I guess that's exactly what I'm saying. Let's go away from here, away from Red and the Red Devil." Jovon was serious. He would take Brittany to see the world and care for her for the rest of her life. All she had to do was say yes. Jovon never thought Red would take a small wager and turn it into a murder plot.

RED

"You need to pack up and get out of there fast! He doesn't know where you are for now. Just to be safe, get out of there now! You know how your brother is; he knows about your daughter and where she is. We have to move fast. Are you good on cash?"
Red knew it would only be a matter of time before Arab found Naomi. Red had all kinds of shady shit going on. Everything was getting out of hand. It seemed Red's castle had begun to crumble. He would

have to pick up the pieces and rebuild his empire if he could not get things under control.

NAOMI

Naomi knew Arab would not give up until he found her. She was going to leave Amsterdam, but she wasn't going to hide anymore. Naomi wanted her daughter and her man. She was tired of running. There was no way she was letting Arab get her hands on her baby. She had to leave Amsterdam and find her baby before it was too late. She knew how Arab's mind worked. He would use her daughter to keep her. And keep his power and control over Naomi. She would rather die than ever have Arab touch her again. He wanted to possess Naomi. He felt he owned her, and she was almost positive he would do the same to her daughter.

RED'S DEVIL'S

ARAB

"What do you mean they are gone!" Arab yelled into his cell phone.

"The house was dark. I went in to check it and the place was empty."

"So, you let them slip through your fingers?"

"They must have gone out the back entrance; it's no sign of them."

"Find them, check hospitals, hotels, and shelters. Check everywhere and find them!" Arab ended the call. Then he punched a hole in his wall and made his fists bleed. He thought there would be plenty more bloodshed, just not his.

AMBER

Amber had to get the hell away from Yields. There was no telling what he was going to try to do to Amber because of his crazy infatuation with her. She thought she was safe because Yields was a police officer, now she felt like she was in even more danger. She thought about going to Canada, where no one would think to look there for her. No one would be looking for her except Red and detective Yields. How did she end up in this crazy situation with two dangerous men pursuing her? She felt as if she had no way out. There was no other alternative; She couldn't run away or stay. She may have to kill Red and probably Yields as well only Amber was no killer. She didn't want to spend the rest of her life in prison. She didn't want to lose everything she had worked so hard to accomplish. Amber had plans for her future. They did not involve running and hiding in Canada or anywhere else. She didn't plan on going anywhere with detective Yield's psychotic ass, and he had talked to her about faking her death. At first Amber did not agree to it. but now, it might just help get out of this dangerous situation. If it worked, she could get her life back on track, or at least back to normal. She would have to get rid of Red, or maybe she would get rid of Red Devil, which would get him off her back. Take from him what he loved the most other than his money. Red Devil was Red's whole world. It made him who he was today. A narcissistic, calculating man with a smile that would melt your heart and a touch that would surely wet your panties. She knew he would not let her walk away.

Amber still had to go to work at the Red Devil until she could set her plan in motion. It made her skin crawl just thinking about walking into the Red Devil. Amber never wanted to see Red's face again, and Yields was waiting for the right time. Amber had to go back to the Red Devil. It was almost time for her shift to start. Going to the club was the last thing she wanted to do. It would only be temporary to feel more in control. Amber called a couple of clients out of her little black book. They would come to the Red Devil to see her. They wouldn't tip any other dancers, and they would not buy any food or drinks. All they did was pay for admission and socialize with Amber. The other devils got upset and complained about what she was doing. Red said he needed to see her before she left; Amber dressed and went to Red's office. She didn't knock. She just walked right in.

"What do you want, Red? I'm tired. I'm ready to go home." Amber rolled her eyes.

RED'S DEVIL'S

"The devils say your friends aren't amiable."

"I'm supposed to give a.fuck?! Tell them to work harder." She turned to walk out the door, but Red grabbed her by her arm." Listen, Ambitious Amber. Or should I call you Angry Amber? I see the game you're playing. I'm telling you now; you won't win." Amber pulled away and pulled her gun out of her bra. "Don't you fucking touch me! I may work here, but that's it. You don't own or brand me; I will never belong to you. You kidnapped me and held me against my will. I will kill you if you ever touch me again."

Red had both hands in the air, laughing at Amber. Then Reece came through the door.

"Is everything ok, Red?" Amber still had her gun pointed at Red.

"It's all good, Reece. I'm sure you have met Ambitious Amber. We were talking. She was leaving." Amber stood there momentarily, then Red-tossed a key to Amber. She caught it with her other hand still pointed to the gun at him.

"What the hell is this?"

RED'S DEVIL'S

He grinned. "You know where to find me when you're ready to play." Amber looked at Reece, then back at Red. She put her gun back in her bra and left the office.

"See you tomorrow." She said over her shoulder and left his office.

BRITTANY

Brittany was on her way to see Red. She noticed Amber walking out of the club, and Fred walked her to her car. Brittany said hello to Fred, then went inside to talk to Red.

"We need to talk." Brittany sat down.

"I swear my door has been revolving all night. You and the whole world fucking with me right now. What have I done to you, Bold Brittany?" Red poured a shot of Hennessy.

"Are you responsible for what happened?" Red looks confused."

"I don't know what you mean, Bold Brittany."

RED'S DEVIL'S

"You do know what the hell I'm talking about, Jovon? You tried to have him killed! Are you fucking crazy!" She stood up and started pacing back and forth.

"Why would I do that?"

"Because you're a psychopath and think you're some god. I don't know why you do the fucked-up shit you do."

"Umm. Calm down. I don't know what you are talking about. I have no beef with Jovon.

I see he has taken an interest in you. I told him you would join the devils and me here at the Red Devil, where you belong. I gave you time to clear your head and come to your senses. I see Jovon has distracted you. I don't have any more time to waste with you and your little plaything. Nobody will make you cum like I did. If you're not here by Monday night, your boy toy might not be so lucky next time." Red was so angry. He smashed the Hennessy bottle into the wall.

"I don't know what planet you are from, but I said no, thank you!" Red grabbed Brittany and kissed her hard on the lips. Britney pulled away and smacked Red in the face.

RED'S DEVIL'S

"You heard me; I will see you Monday." Red pushed Britney toward the door.

" Don't fucking touch me, you asshole. Touch me again; I will fucking kill you!"

"Nothing turns me on more than seeing you angry." He kissed Britney as she walked out of his office. Red thought long and hard of what he would do to her the next time he saw her." I will hear you breathing in my ear when I make you feel good." He whispered.

BIG PAPA

Big Papa received a call from his terrified sister, explaining how she had to run with Big Papa's daughter because of a strange man sitting outside her house watching them. Now she did not feel safe. Kathy checked in with a fake ID so no one could track her down quickly. He could not contact Lisa and wasn't ready to deal with Arab. That's one bullet he was trying to dodge.

RED'S DEVIL'S

JOVON

Jovon still couldn't believe Red would try to have him killed. It could not have been anyone else other than Red. Brittany didn't look like the type to have a crazy ex running around with a gun. He told them may the best man win. Seriously! Jovon shook his head and rubbed his arm. What kind of fight to the deaf shit is this? Jovon knew what he had to do. Somebody needed to beat some sense into Red and bring him back to reality. Jovon always thought Red was a little off, or as the rich say, he was a little eccentric but this time he crossed the line, Seriously, having someone try to kill him that's an unforgivable sin. No way Jovon was going to let him get away with that shit. It's not like Red and Brittany were together. She didn't have a ring on her finger. Red must be out of his mind. Jovon knew things about Red but he didn't know he had gotten this diabolical. Jovon was not about to let Red get a second chance to try to take him out.

RED'S DEVIL'S

REECE

Someone had tried or threatened Red's life more than once. Lisa is nowhere to be found, and Dara killed her ex in self-defense. At the same time, Red held Amber against her will, Detective Yields is up to something, Fred got jumped, and Arab knows about Naomi and Big Papa having a 5-year-old daughter. All the pieces are still not fitting together yet in the puzzle. She needed to do some more digging and check a few traps. Red had more than one target on his back. Reece was determined to find out who and why.

AMBER

Amber pulled up to her loft and saw that detective Yields was waiting for her. She was so glad she had her gun loaded and ready. She knew she had to play it cool.

" I was worried about you." Detective Yields walked up to Amber, hugged her, and tried to kiss her, and she turned her head

"Hey you, I'm just tired. Can I call you tomorrow?" Her head was pounding so was her heart. "Are you sure you don't want to have a nightcap? A few orgasms will cure any headache. I love the way our bodies fit together. I told you we were meant to be." Detective Yields tried to kiss Amber again. She turned her head again.

"Please, I'm sorry. I have a terrible headache. I will call you tomorrow." Amber led him to the door. Then she closed it and locked it. She pulled her gun from her bra and set it on the dining room table. She sat down and blew out a long, deep breath. She had never been so scared in her life.

YIELDS

RED'S DEVIL'S

Yields got in his car, opened his tablet, and pulled up the footage inside Amber's house. She had no clue that he had hidden cameras all over her house. He went to the bathroom camera and jacked off while watching Amber shower. Amber had no idea she was starring in her own movie, directed by Detective Yields.

KATHY

Kathy knew how to live off the grid. She was engaged to a ex-cop, who was an extremist. He taught her how to exist without existing. Matt died in a tragic mountain climbing accident on a trip to Paris, France. After his death, Kathy never left Paris. Instead, she stayed connected with Big Pappa, and that's how Red found her. Big Pappa put her down as an emergency contact in his paperwork. She wished she had never answered the phone five years ago. It was a phone call that was about to change the course of everyone's lives.

RED'S DEVIL'S

RED

Red was tired of everyone threatening his life, blaming him for their bullshit. The Red Devil was a world he created for himself. He showed a lot of pride in how well he groomed Lisa into his perfect devil, the one devil that would always be by his side. Those days are long gone. He didn't want to think about the Red Devil without Lisa there. He didn't want to lose her or Willow. If Lisa found them, she would surely take Willow somewhere far away, and Red would never see either of them again. He refused to bow down to anybody. This was his world. He was the king of the castle, the master of the universe. He did what he wanted. He didn't care who got hurt. He wouldn't let anyone get in his way to get what he wanted.

RED'S DEVIL'S

AMBER

Amber was still wrapped in her bath towel; Her hair was wet from the shower. She sat on the bed and pulled Yields file out of her purse. She started reading the documents and wondered how he ever became a police officer? He had harassment charges, assault, stalking, mandatory counseling, and psych meds and AA meetings. He was a complete basket case. A basket case she thought she was falling in love with. Amber put the file down on the bed and checked all the doors and windows to make sure they were locked. Then she put her gun under her pillow, while Yields watched her every move.

ARAB

Arab made a bad judgment call by waiting to go after Naomi's daughter. He wanted to bring Naomi home first, then get his niece and be a family. After that, he would marry Naomi and raise her and Big Papa's child as his own. Kathy may have slipped away for the moment, but he was nowhere near done with Red or Big Papa.

BIG PAPA

He knew Kathy could handle herself, but that didn't stop him from worrying. He felt terrible for how he dealt with the news, especially since she did all of this for him. They were always close and promised to take care of each other. Neither of them had a good relationship with their other brothers and sisters. He was like the black sheep of the boys, and she was the black sheep of the girls, so they always stuck together. He knew Kathy would do anything for him and his daughter. Kathy had prayed for five years that she would never get that call from Red. Kathy prepared for that day; she would be ready when he called. His voice was the last one she wanted to hear on the other end of her phone. Big Poppa felt helpless during the whole situation. He knew he had to be careful and watch his back. Big Papa didn't know who to trust. He knew he wanted to be with his daughter and find her mother. Maybe it was time to leave the Red Devil. He could work anywhere in the country with his skills. That would not be a problem. He would be able to support his family and keep them safe but he would need some help. He knew he couldn't do it alone.

NAOMI

Naomi got cold chills thinking about seeing Arab again. It was time she faced him. She wasn't a little girl anymore. She would have to stand up to Arab once and for all. Her child's life depended on it as well as Big Papa's. She was willing to sacrifice herself to save Big Papa and their daughter. At least he could raise their child. If it meant going back to Arab, then that's what she would have to do.

RED'S DEVIL'S

YIELDS

"She knows! She knows, damn it! Did you give her that file? How did she get that? You gave it to her. You promised you would keep my secret as I kept yours." His hands were shaking; he was pacing the floor.

"Now you want to talk after you put a gun in my face for a woman you had no permission to pursue. I paid you to watch and persuade her to be a devil and work for me. Then you go off your meds, and boom! You're in love. You found your soul mate." Red made Yields a drink.

"Listen, this has nothing to do with my meds, damn it! She is my soul mate, and I love her. You don't love anybody so you wouldn't understand. Anyway, she knows the truth now. She won't go! She won't go. She is like the other liars and users, thinking they're too good for me. Like I don't deserve a beautiful woman. Like I don't work hard for my money. Well, I got news for her. She's not better than me." Yields downed to his drink and slammed the glass on Red's desk.

"You have nothing to worry about; she is a devil now. She is no longer your problem, so go out there and pick yourself a new soul mate. Go home and take your medication. I need you at your best. Something big is coming up, and I need you ready." Red poured him another drink.

"I told you I am in love with her. Just let me have her. There are millions of women out here that you can have. Instead, you treat me like I'm an idiot or something. I told you, Red, you can't have her. This isn't over."

Yield stormed out of the office, kicked down the flowerpot, and punched a mirror. He was not going to let Red take Amber away from him. Red tried to sabotage their relationship by giving her that file of lies. Now she would think he was crazy like the rest of those stupid bitches. They laughed at him, turned him down, and betrayed him; they hurt him. They deserved to die. No one makes a fool out of him. Why couldn't they love him back? He never meant to hurt anyone. It was their fault. They made him do it. All he tried to do was show them how much he loved him, but they wouldn't let him

REECE

Reece was in the kitchen while Big Papa was in the restroom. She removed the bug she had planted and snuck back out without being seen. She knew Red was out, so he wouldn't be watching the cameras in his office. The first time she was in Red's office, he took her to the toy box. He made her strip down, then strapped her to the bed, spread eagle, and blindfolded her. Red kissed Reece's breasts and sucked her nipples. Then he licked Reece clit then kissed her lips. Reece was moaning and wiggling around. She could feel herself about to cum and the devil stopped. After Reece came, he kissed her then gave her a full-body massage. Red was rubbing her whole body down, then kissing and licking every curve of her body. She came back-to-back thrice, then

RED'S DEVIL'S

Red unstrapped her legs and arms, flipped her over on all fours, and handcuffed her hands behind her back. He took the blindfold off. Red sucked her pussy from the back and slapped her ass. Then he got an anal vibrator and slid it in her ass while he fucked her from the back. Reese came so hard she thought she would pass out for sure. He uncuffed her and flipped her over again. This time, Reese rolled on top of Red and did the splits while riding his dick. She rode his dick like a champion until he came. Red painted her face with his cum. When Red went to shower, Reece made her move and planted the camera and microphone. Then she went to join Red the devil in the rain for round two.

BIG PAPA

Big Papa arrived at the Red Devil early. He had to do something from driving himself crazy. When he walked into the kitchen, he thought he smelled Naomi's Authentic Religion perfume. It was her favorite and his too. He loved how good she used to smell. Big Papa entered his office to make up the daily menu and found a note on his computer monitor. It was written on a post-it with an address, the time, and the date. Big Papa put the post-it in his wallet and continued preparing his food.

ARAB

Arab pulled up on Amber outside of EBO's Bar and restaurant.

"Excuse me, miss; we need to talk." Amber walked toward EBO's, and Arab got out of his car.

"I'm not interested." Amber said with an attitude.

"I think you will be very interested in what I have to say. We both have the same enemy, our mutual acquaintance Red." That stopped Amber in her tracks.

"What about Red? Amber asked Arab?"

RED'S DEVIL'S

"I know what Red has been doing to you, forcing you to be a devil: you don't belong there. You know that, and so does he. Red has completely lost his mind, and he's becoming a tyrant. He needs to be put in his place. He doesn't play well with others. He is a thorn in my ass, like a mad dog that needs to be put down."

"Even if all that is true, what do you want from me?"

"Maybe we can help each other eliminate our problem and return to living peacefully and set Red free."

Amber didn't know what the hell he was getting to."
Listen, I don't know who you are and what you want from me, but I'm not interested."

"Wait, just wait. Red is after you, and Yields is obsessed with you. If I'm not mistaken, you have two unstable men chasing you. It seems to me they aren't going to leave you alone. Red will try to control you and take over your life. Then you will be stuck in The Red Devil until you age out or married to some unstable nut job that might kill you because he is so in love with you. You want to live your prime days stuck in The Red Devils, following Red's ridiculous rules, and living like a slave. You don't seem like the type to be brainwashed and branded. Let's help one another to resolve our problem."

Arab took Amber's phone and removed the back of the case to expose a battery and remove the small chip. It was a tracking device. Her phone was being tracked as well. He threw it on the ground and stepped on it.

"Go home and check for cameras and hidden microphones."

Arab handed Amber a new cell phone and told her to call him on that phone only. He would call her soon and discuss how they would handle Red. If Red wanted to play games, he had better prepare because judgment day was coming. Arab has something planned for Red. He would keep it to himself. He wouldn't get his hands dirty until he knew Amber would be on board. As long as the job gets done. Amber might not be the one to help him, but he was hoping she wanted to get rid of Red just as much as Arab did. Arab knew there was no way Red would let her walk away from him. Amber didn't know what she was up against. If she wanted to be rid of Red, she would need Arab's help. He knew more about Red than she did. Was she built for this kind of shit? If she wasn't, she better get ready, time was running out for everyone involved. Arab knew Amber was desperate, and the only way for her to be rid of Red was if she helped Arab. He hoped she would come to her senses and realize Arab was the only hope. He was right; Red would not let go. She would belong to him. Red would pay even if Amber didn't agree to help him with his plan to care for Red. Arab needed to find Naomi. Red was the only person who knew where she was, and he wasn't talking.

Made in the USA
Middletown, DE
08 February 2024